Help! Someone's Died

Help! Someone's Died
Finding a Way Through Bereavement

Mary Sim

Illustrations by Jeanette Turner

Help! Someone's Died: Finding a Way Through Bereavement
Mary Sim

Published by Aspect Design 2018
Malvern, Worcestershire, United Kingdom.

Designed, printed and bound by Aspect Design
89 Newtown Road, Malvern, Worcs. WR14 1PD
United Kingdom
Tel: 01684 561567
E-mail: allan@aspect-design.net
Website: www.aspect-design.net

ISBN 978-1-912078-58-5

Contents

Chapter One
The Beginning

Saturday. The phone rings.

'Is that Ian Sim?'

'It is.'

'Are you the father of Daniel Sim?'

'Yes.'

'This is —— police here. I'm sorry to tell you that your son Daniel has been found dead at his home. We'll be with you in about forty minutes.'

'He can't be dead,' I said, 'I saw him on Wednesday . . . I spent the day with him . . . we had a lovely day . . .'

We sat in silence, each of us lost in our own thoughts. We couldn't take it in. I watched as the minutes on the clock moved slowly round.

Daniel had been in good form when I last saw him. He had been looking forward to starting his new job . . . he'd even shaved his beard off in readiness for it. How could he be dead?

But he was.

So continued my journey with grief or what is sometimes referred to as walking through the valley of the shadow of death. It had begun a few months earlier with the death of my mother, who had been suffering from stroke-related dementia for several years. Then several weeks later a very close friend who, with her husband, had been like a third set of grandparents to our children, died after a fall. I feel that it is only since that time that I have begun to fully understand how such losses can impact on so many areas of a person's life. The death of a loved one has been described as 'one of the most intensely painful experiences any human being can suffer.' Yet it encompasses so much more that just a feeling of great sadness and pain at the loss.

Walking through this valley may feel like being in a new country with no compass or destination. Are we properly equipped to cope with this journey? Sometimes the clouds lift and give rise to sunshine for a while. Often the path seems rough and steep but will then even out and become smooth and flat for some distance. Occasionally it feels as though there are obstacles to contend with, or that we have to fight our way through dense undergrowth. The terrain or weather may take us by surprise and leave us feeling ill-prepared. There may be hidden dangers along the way. The valley may seem dark with no light at the end.

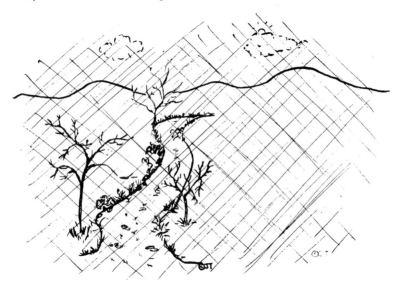

I believe that we can experience all those things and that it is a lonely journey.

> Susan received much support from friends when her ten-year-old son, Joe, was suffering from a tumour. However, after his death most of that support gradually came to an end and Susan felt that she was very much alone in her grief.

The need to know that there are those walking with us is so important even in our aloneness. We may be fortunate enough to have friends or family who will walk alongside us and give comfort, encouragement and support. However, no-one walks in our shoes.

> I know two other mothers whose children died in similar circumstances to Daniel, so we may think that we understand each other's grief. Yes, we've all suffered the death of one of our children, but we don't know what effect their death has had on each of us. Their personalities were different and our relationship with them was different. Even though each of us knows what it is like to lose a child, we can't experience the feelings of others. Our feelings are unique to us as was the relationship we had with our child.

Ian and I grieve together for the same son, but even our journeys are different: we have our own issues and emotions to deal with. Our relationships with Daniel were different: Ian was not his mother and I was not his father, so how can we know what it is like for each other? I am so grateful to Alison who, out of her own experience, warned us that we might react differently and that we must allow each other to grieve in the way that was right for each of us. One person may need to sit quietly, while another may need to keep busy. We haven't travelled this way before but we navigate the route as best as we can.

There are many ways in which grief affects us that are not spoken about. They are what I think of as the hidden dangers of walking through the valley. Talking with other people since Daniel died has raised comments such as, 'I thought that's what I was expected to do,' or 'I had no idea it would be like this.' We talk about closure, resolution, recovery, getting over the death and completing the process. Yet how does that fit with knowing that even twenty years after the death of a loved one, the relative can still be reduced to tears at an unexpected reminder of the person? In conversation with bereaved people, I have found that even after many years they are still quick to bring up issues that were a difficulty for them at the time. The feelings they had then are often still close to the surface, and they describe them as if the death has only recently occurred.

Nearly eight years after her brother-in-law's death, Rebecca still remembered:

> 'When friends came round the day after he died, we were putting our arms round *them*, reassuring *them*. It was bizarre because they should have been comforting *us*.'

Do we ever feel that we have had closure or are there some wounds that will never completely heal?

Our friend John made a very helpful comment to one of our boys at Daniel's funeral. He comforted us with, 'life will get back to normal, but normal will be different.' Nearly eleven years later I can say that our lives are normal again. However, life is not the same as it was, because one member of our family is missing. It can never go back to how it was before. Parents do not expect to bury their children, so there is a different kind of adjustment from when a parent or elderly person dies. The experience of any death may cause us to feel that we have become different people, because of how it has affected us.

Two years after Daniel's death I studied for a degree, which included a module on loss and bereavement. I also undertook some small-scale research on a related topic. I read literature about what are often referred to as stages of grief, which has helped my understanding of the process: particularly of what happens to our emotions after such an event. However, most of us do not read these books, and even if we do, we may be confused if we don't experience all the stages mentioned. We may be left wondering if how we are feeling or how we are coping is 'normal'. Our lives do not always fit into neat little boxes and so we are left with questions. Do other people feel like this? Do other people ask the questions I am asking? Should I be able to do this by now? Should I have 'got over it' and be 'moving on' with my life? I hope that some of these questions will be answered as you read this book.

There are myths surrounding death, and its customs, which are not discussed openly, so that we often assume what is expected of us. This can become an added pressure as we try to conform to these expectations. Friends may offer advice that, although well-meaning, is not always helpful. However there may also be occasions when we find ourselves saying, 'I wish someone had told me that.' So how do we manage our grief when there is no magic formula for getting us through it? There is no one at our side saying each day, 'you're doing well: keep going.' How do friends know the best way to help us on our journey? We may be so wrapped up in ourselves and our grief that they do not feel they are 'getting through' to us.

I hope that what I have learned, through my research and from talking with many bereaved people while Ian was a church minister and GP surgery counsellor for forty years, will be of value to you as you read this book. I haven't got all the answers and I know that my experience is limited. There seem to be no right or wrong answers to dealing with grief. We all cope with it in different ways. So I invite you to come with me on my personal journey and together we will join with others on the same path. As you walk with me I hope you will gain some insight into the outworking of grief, whether it be your own or that of someone who needs you by their side.

Chapter Two
Organising the Funeral

The days immediately following the death are difficult to describe. It may be a time of feeling 'in limbo,' especially while waiting for the funeral to take place. You may still be in shock, particularly if the death was sudden and unexpected. You may feel a kind of 'nothingness'. You can't believe it has happened and you keep thinking you will wake up the next morning and find it has all been a dream. On the other hand, you may feel completely overwhelmed by your emotions, and feel that you will never stop crying. You may wonder how you're going to get through this pain and loss.

Even while all this is happening, there is usually a funeral to plan. The funeral is a gathering of people who wish to show their respect or love for the person who has died. The person who leads the funeral, and maybe family members or friends, will say words that help us remember them. Words may also be said to bring comfort. Hymns may be sung and prayers said if it is a religious service. The leader will say words that commit the body for burial or cremation. The executor or person responsible for organising the funeral needs to be aware that instructions may have been left regarding the funeral.

When a wedding is being planned it often takes many weeks or even months to organise. A venue has to be found for the service or ceremony, flowers ordered and the reception catered for. Invitations need to be sent out, wedding clothes bought and so on. Although there may be some stress involved there is the knowledge that it will all come together for what will be a happy occasion.

Arranging a funeral is, in some ways, very similar. The venue needs to be found, people have to be informed, often by word of mouth or putting a notice in the local newspaper. Catering may need to be organised, flowers ordered and suitable clothes decided upon. Often people in the UK wear black clothes to a funeral. This is a tradition that goes back to Roman times, although it is not so rigidly kept to now. Other countries have different colours for mourning. Sometimes instructions have been left that colourful clothes are to be worn at the funeral. However, compared with a wedding, the time scale is very different. Usually there will only be a week or two in which to organise everything. Whoever is responsible for the arrangements may find this difficult as their emotions may be 'all over the place'. They may not be able to think logically. Later on, they may wish they had done things differently. They may have made different choices if they had been thinking clearly.

So it may be helpful for someone not so emotionally close to the deceased person to take on some of the practical tasks that need doing. This could be ordering the flowers or cars, or making phone calls.

Sometimes the deceased person has planned their own funeral service. This is often when the person has had a terminal illness, or it may happen among older folk who realise they are getting towards the end of their lives. There are those who find this idea rather morbid, so we need to try to understand this from the viewpoint of the one facing death.

They may have specific ideas about funerals and they want to know that their own one will be as they would like it to be. This may be particularly so where the person has a faith and members of their family do not, or the other way round.

> Eve had a very strong Christian faith and knew that her daughter was an atheist. It was important to her to know that her faith and God would be central to the service, so her daughter respected her wishes.
>
> Paula had rejected her Christian upbringing and specified that she did not want a Christian funeral.

Organising one's own funeral may help to relieve the stress on the family, especially if members of the family have different ideas on what they would like. It also allows for the inclusion of something personal to the one who has died. For instance, a wife may want a particular song or piece of music that was special to her and her husband. The person may want to include something they know will be helpful or meaningful to those who will attend the service. There may also be a feeling of comfort, knowing that everything is in order, ready for when they die.

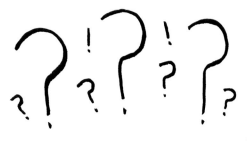

Maybe at this point it would be helpful to think about why we have funerals. Secular funerals usually refer to the 'ceremony' whereas religious ones usually refer to the 'service,' which is the word I am using to include both. Are we brought up to believe that having a funeral is just what we do in that situation, and so we do not question it?

Several years ago I met a lady who had terminal cancer and she had made it known that she did not want a funeral. I found the whole idea quite upsetting, and wondered why. Was it because I felt that a funeral was one way to 'say goodbye' when there had been no other opportunity? Perhaps a funeral is a way of showing respect and giving dignity to the one who has died. Without one, does it seem as if no-one cared for the person who has died? For me I think it was a mixture of all those reasons. How did the lady concerned view the purpose of a funeral? Was it that 'once

I am gone it is not important what happens afterwards'? Maybe we feel as she did. Our answers to these questions may help us determine our own thoughts about funerals. If we are responsible for organising one, we will then be able to think about how to make the service appropriate for those who mourn, as well as for the one who has died. If there is to be no service, the funeral director will make all the necessary arrangements for the burial or cremation.

There are those who believe that it takes much longer for someone to come to terms with a death where there is no funeral ritual, no coffin to cry over or ceremony to go through. Years ago, parents who had still-births did not always have a funeral. Families of those who die abroad are not always able to attend the funeral. The same may apply to people in prison or in hospital, when someone they love dies. A thanksgiving service at a later date may help, but some people find it difficult not having a coffin there. Maybe seeing the coffin is part of accepting the reality of the death. In the same way, others find it hard to accept that someone has died if they do not see the body. Depending on the circumstances, this is not always possible, as for example, with those who die at sea.

Ian, in his work as a counsellor and church minister, has conducted what we might call a 'substitute service' for those who were deprived of the funeral of a loved one. He has seen how even when this takes place years later, it seems to have a positive and healing benefit: enabling the person to then move on with their lives in a way they couldn't before.

We often hear people saying they were so glad to see the deceased person after they had died because they looked so peaceful. This may counteract having a memory of how they looked when they were in pain. Others prefer to remember their loved one as they were when they were well, and not as they looked after death. This may be particularly so if there has been an accident or a violent death.

I found it upsetting to see how Daniel looked in the mortuary when we had to go and identify his body. When we came home, we put up lots of photos of him smiling. Then whenever I remembered how he looked in the mortuary I would look at the photos to try to erase that image.

The various ideas and wishes concerning funerals may mean that it is not be possible to please everyone. Some family members and close friends may have to work through their own feelings, and come to terms with their differences.

Fran struggled with knowing that her mother had asked to be cremated and yet other members of the family decided that she should be buried. How would she come to terms with knowing that her mother's wishes had not been respected? Would she be able to let it go, knowing that life had ended for her mother and so the decision could not hurt her?

Then there is the question: should children attend funerals? Many older people relate personal stories from their childhood: they were not told when someone had died or they were not told about the funeral. Even if they were told, the attitude of those days was generally that funerals were not for children. Death was a taboo subject, shrouded in mystery. Today many of those same people will talk about the emotional harm they feel from not being told of the death, or not being allowed to go to the funeral. Some are still trying to come to terms with it, even forty or fifty years later on. On the other hand, there are children who were made to look at the dead body of someone close and that can also leave lasting harmful images. Most parents will do what they feel is best for their children, but it is helpful to take all the various issues into consideration. When children are very young then obviously the parents will make this decision. My own opinion is that as they get older, they can make their own decisions, if the subject is openly and sensitively discussed. When Ian's mother died, our two older children did not wish to attend the funeral whereas the younger two did. We respected their wishes.

Peter received criticism from friends, who thought it was not right that his two young children attended their grandmother's funeral.

Children need to grieve just as adults do; and they need that opportunity to say 'goodbye' in the way that is right for them.

When planning a wedding the couple may be told, 'this is *your* wedding, *your* day.' Similarly those close relatives who organise the funeral should be able to feel that it is appropriate for them and the person who has died. It is 'their' day. Favourite songs may be played before or after the service. Video recordings of special events in the life of the deceased person may be shown on screen. Photos of the person's life may be on display.

Sometimes people are so distressed or in such a state of shock that afterwards they have no recollection of the funeral. Others appear to be 'on a high,' with no outward appearance of upset. During the service, a member of the family may speak about the person who has died and I have heard people say, 'I couldn't do that, I would be too upset.' If a loss of control does happen, the person concerned is usually able to regain their composure and everyone understands. However there are times when the person does become too upset to continue, so it is helpful to have a 'contingency plan'. Ian always has a copy of what is being read in case he needs to step in and take over. We need to acknowledge that we are all different, and we have our own individual ways of coping and paying our respects. We all react differently to situations, particularly when our emotions are involved. However, as far as is possible at such an occasion, the funeral needs to be of help and comfort to those who mourn.

There is a sense in which the funeral is an ending and a beginning. It is an ending of life for the person who has died. For those who mourn, it is the end of the life they have had together with that person. Life will never be the same as it was before. On the other hand, the funeral also marks the beginning of a journey into unknown territory. It is a lonely path, for even when surrounded and supported by friends and family, grieving is something we have to work through on our own and in our own way.

Chapter Three
Practical Considerations

Having thought about the funeral service, it may be helpful to look at some of the practicalities that may be involved before and afterwards. Differing arrangements and ways can be chosen to mark the death of a loved one. We do not have to conform to a set pattern.

However some things are not negotiable before a funeral can be arranged. A medical certificate, stating the cause of death, has to be obtained from the doctor. This enables you to register the death at the local registry office. This needs to be done within five days of the death in England and Wales. In Scotland it needs to be within eight days. The registrar will issue you with the documents needed to arrange the funeral. Extra copies of the death certificate are useful when dealing with financial and government departments.

If it is not clear why the person died, the doctor will probably refer the death to a coroner, who may ask for a post-mortem to be held. The coroner will release the body for the funeral once the post-mortem is completed and no further examinations are needed.

If the deceased person has left instructions for their body to be donated for medical science, the medical school will usually arrange for the body to be cremated. However, the family can still request the return of the body for a private burial or cremation.

In this country there is usually a week or more between the death and the funeral; and this can be a difficult time. Although there are many things to sort out, it may feel rather like sitting in a waiting room. Alternatively it may be helpful in giving time for what has happened, to sink in.

Carol appreciated being able to see her sister in the chapel of rest several times before the funeral took place. It helped her to grasp what had happened and was a comfort to be able to see her looking peaceful after a difficult time.

On the other hand, for others, the reality of the death may not be realised until the funeral takes place.

In most British culture the rituals and customs surrounding death have all but disappeared. At one time there was a community-grieving. The body would lie in the coffin in the house for friends and neighbours to pay their respects.

Someone may have sat with the deceased person, keeping vigil until the funeral took place. Curtains were always drawn in the houses in the street where the deceased had lived. On the day of the funeral, neighbours and work colleagues would line the street as the hearse went past. Those in mourning wore black clothes or arm-bands, so everyone would know that they were grieving: they didn't have to keep explaining. Today most people die in hospital, hospices or nursing homes and are then taken to a chapel of rest at the funeral directors. So, although some people do still die at home, death is not as much a part of life as it used to be. It is almost hidden away. Some religions or cultures encourage crying and displaying their grief in public. We tend to suppress our tears in front of other people. Is this because we are not sure how people will react: or do we think we have to 'keep a stiff upper lip'?

Having these customs gave a certain structure to help in the grieving process, whereas today people are not sure what is expected of them. They don't always know how to behave. It may be that new rituals are evolving, such as balloons being released and petals thrown in the sea. Flowers are often left at the roadside when a fatal accident has occurred. Messages of love and condolences, flowers or other items are also often left near the home or school of someone who has died. This allows us to express our grief in a collective way, particularly in the case of a well-known figure such as Princess Diana.

I mentioned earlier how different religions and cultures have their own traditions for grieving. Their funerals may be very different from the ones we are used to. They need to be respected. However I am focussing on Christian or secular funerals and continue to use the word 'service' to include 'ceremony'.

A funeral is a public acknowledgement that a life has been lived and a death has now occurred. The body may be buried or cremated.

The rigidity of the funeral service has changed over the years. There is much more flexibility and choice about the form these can take. Some people think that there are set procedures for services, which is not so. There is also confusion about who is allowed to conduct a funeral service. If it is a secular one, there are no rules as to who can officiate. However in the case of a religious funeral, the particular religious leader will need to be contacted to find out their procedure.

Those who were close to the person who has died need to feel comfortable with the funeral arrangements. It is usual to organise the funeral through a funeral director. Funerals today are not only conducted in church or crematorium. Woodland and Green funerals are becoming popular, particularly with those concerned about conservation issues. For others it is the appeal of knowing their loved one is in a beautiful and peaceful setting.

The format of the funeral will vary according to personal preference. There may be a service in a church, followed by the burial in the church graveyard. Other people may have a service at the crematorium, and then hold a 'celebration-of-life' gathering or thanksgiving service in another venue. This may be on the same day or weeks later. Alternatively there may be a service at a Woodland burial site. There is no set procedure that has to be followed.

Paula's funeral was at the local crematorium, followed straight afterwards by a celebration-of-life gathering at a nearby hotel.

Edna had her father's funeral service at the local church and then the body was driven to be buried in the family grave some hundred miles away.

If the service is at a crematorium, it is helpful to remember that the time allowed is usually fairly short. This may mean that you are limited in what you can include. If you wish to sing, check whether they have an instrument and musician available. They may use recorded music.

After cremation, the ashes may be buried or scattered. This may be in a Garden of Remembrance at a church or cemetery, or at some other burial site. Some of the Green burial grounds will not allow the burial of ashes. Alternatively, the family may wish them to be scattered or buried at a place of significance for them or the deceased person. This may be done with a formal service or ceremony or the family may wish to do it themselves. Always check that scattering of ashes is permissible in public places as there are sometimes environmental issues to consider. Some people keep the ashes in a container in their own home.

> Carol scattered her mother's ashes in the sea where they had spent many happy family holidays.
>
> Pam scattered her mother's ashes in her own garden.

Usually the funeral service is held in the place where the deceased person lived. However, deciding where to bury the body or scatter the ashes can sometimes cause a dilemma for the

15

family. It is also worth while finding out whether the burial place is guaranteed not to be disturbed or built upon in the future, thus causing more distress.

Although my mother had died shortly before Daniel, we had not yet decided what to do with her ashes, as other members of the family were involved. Where should the burial or scattering of ashes be when someone has moved away from their home town yet other members of the family are buried there? This sometimes occurs when an elderly person has moved to be near one of their children after their partner has died. Would it be best for them to be buried in the same place as other members of their family? Sometimes family members are living, or have been buried, in different parts of the country, so there is no one place that would suit everyone. We eventually decided to have my mother's ashes buried where my father's ashes are: not near any of her children.

> Elizabeth, whose mother came to live with her after the death of her father, had a similar dilemma. However she did not take the ashes back to where her father's were buried. Her mother had never been back after moving and she had been very happy living with her daughter. So Elizabeth placed items that had belonged to her father and her grandparents in the coffin with her mother. This brought a sense of family togetherness. The ashes were buried at the church Elizabeth attended. She was then able to put flowers there regularly. The names of both her parents are inscribed in the Books of Remembrance in both places, symbolically uniting them again.

Added distress may be caused for parents when an adult married child dies. The spouse and/or children may not want them to be involved in organising the funeral. Parents may find it difficult not being able to make decisions about someone they still think of as 'their child'.

> Joan wanted to have a say in the planning of the funeral service of her daughter: but her son-in-law did not want to involve her.

Edward and Shirley would have liked a say in what happened to their son's ashes, but his partner had her own ideas and did not involve them.

The funeral arrangements may be seen as the last loving gesture towards the person who has died, as well as the chance to say 'goodbye'. Although the funeral may be thought of as an ending and a 'letting go,' we continue to remember them and hold them in our hearts.

Chapter Four
Daniel's Funeral

We had to wait quite a while for Daniel's funeral. There had to be a post-mortem, because the death was sudden and the cause was not known. We did not get the results for several months and that was an additional stress. We held the funeral not knowing why he had died. We were not able to give an answer when friends and family wanted to know how he had died.

> 'I was sorry to hear that Daniel had died. Had he been ill?'
> 'No.'
> 'Was he involved in an accident?'
> 'No.'
> Pause.
> 'We don't know why he died.'
> Awkward silence.

The preparations for Daniel's funeral began with a visit from the funeral director. We had no idea of Daniel's wishes so we tried to make the funeral arrangements helpful to the family and also honouring his character and nature.

We were asked if we wanted to take Daniel's own clothes to dress him in for the funeral. When we had seen him in the mortuary he was dressed in what looked like a white gown which seemed quite inappropriate. Yet my immediate response was to think, 'What difference does it make when he's dead? That's not Daniel, it's just his body.' So we left him as he was.

Many months later I thought, 'We should have put his own clothes on him, the ones he would have felt comfortable in.' In hindsight I felt that we had been disrespectful to him. As I write this I know that there was nothing wrong with my initial reasoning but when the shock wore off, it did not feel right on an emotional level.

The day before Daniel's funeral we had been with three very special friends to sit with his coffin in the chapel of rest. His brothers and their wives did not want to come. I haven't got words to describe how distraught I felt. Looking back now, I think that having that time, when I could 'be myself,' enabled me to cope with the following day. Maybe I had already said my 'goodbye'.

Then the day of the funeral arrived. We asked friends to take us to the crematorium rather than travel in funeral cars with strangers.

We had decided to have Daniel cremated at our local crematorium, after which we held a thanksgiving service at our church, followed by refreshments. We did it in this order so people who did not wish to come to the crematorium would not have to wait for refreshments till we got back. I think I would have found the thanksgiving service harder to cope with if I had known that the final parting at the crematorium was still to come.

Usually at a crematorium, curtains are drawn round the coffin at the end of the service and the family mourners leave first. However we wanted our last few moments with Daniel to be private and personal.

> We asked everyone else to leave first so that we had time on our own at the end. The curtains were left open and we were able to gather round the coffin together and say 'goodbye'.

Daniel was not interested in flowers but he loved mountain biking, so one of our sons had made a wire framework of a bike. A friend decorated it with greenery to remind us of the forest where Daniel lived and cycled. This was put on the willow coffin. Willow seemed more appropriate for him than a traditional wooden one.

When we arrived at the church hall we put the bike, his dirty old cap which was like his 'trade mark' and a bottle of beer from the brewery, where he had previously worked, on a table at the front. We felt that they were symbolic of Daniel and his personality. It is important that the service is personal to the family and not necessarily what we think other people will expect. Like many people do now, we had photos of him displayed for friends and family to look at and recall times past.

We had planned the service together as a family, with everyone having some input. Ian and I wrote a tribute to Daniel. His brothers and their wives wrote collectively. The hall was packed with family and friends and we felt 'carried along' by their love and support for us as we remembered his life.

Afterwards, we invited everyone to stay for refreshments which gave us an opportunity to talk with friends and family, some of whom had travelled long distances.

Ian and I had made the decision to have Daniel cremated without discussing it with his brothers. It would have been helpful

to them if we had, but it didn't occur to us at the time. None of them had voiced an opinion. Often when we are in shock or upset we do not think logically, or we overlook certain practicalities completely. It was not until we came to discussing what to do with Daniel's ashes that we discovered the difficulty it had caused. We learned that one member of our family had struggled with the concept of cremation. This then gave rise to further discussion as to whether to scatter or bury his ashes. It felt particularly important that this should be a decision to suit everyone. At the time, I felt that I could not cope with the thought of burying the ashes. I did not want to know 'where Daniel was' even though I knew that it was not 'him.' I also had this picture in my head of grieving people not being able to stay away from the grave and it becoming the focus of their lives. I think there was a fear that would happen to me. No-one else had strong views either way. So, trying to take everyone's thoughts and feelings into account, we eventually decided to bury Daniel's ashes. This seemed a compromise on the burial or cremation issue. So some time later we took the ashes to the cemetery near his home. We invited one of his special friends, who he had known since Playgroup days, to join us. Ian said a few words and prayed, and together, as a family, we buried his ashes and said our final 'goodbye' to him.

It became clear that we had made the right decision, as some of us, including me, visit the cemetery from time to time. This is meaningful for each of us in different ways. We also know of one of Daniel's friends who visits.

We have been asked why we did not bury Daniel's ashes near our own home. He had told us that he never wanted to move from the town where he lived. So to bury them at the crematorium near his home, in the forest he loved so much, seemed a way of respecting his wishes. The small plaque we have there says simply 'At home in the forest'. Daniel would have liked that.

Remember

Remember me when I am gone away,
    Gone far away into the silent land;
    When you can no more hold me by the hand,
Nor I half turn to go yet turning stay.
Remember me when no more day by day
    You tell me of our future that you plann'd:
    Only remember me; you understand
It will be late to counsel then or pray.
Yet if you should forget me for a while
    And afterwards remember, do not grieve:
    For if the darkness and corruption leave
A vestige of the thoughts that once I had,
Better by far you should forget and smile
    Than that you should remember and be sad.

(Christina Rossetti)

Chapter Five
Formalities

Following a death, there are certain formalities and legalities that have to be dealt with. In previous chapters we have looked at certifying and registering the death, and the need for a coroner to be involved for sudden and unexplained deaths. There are other reasons why a doctor may refer a death to the coroner. Information on this and many other issues concerned with a death, can be found on the government website. There is too much to include here.

Following a post-mortem, there may need to be be an inquest which could be months later as it was for us. An inquest is held if the cause of death was not known, or the person has died from a violent or unnatural death. The purpose of an inquest is to find out who died: when, where, how and in what circumstances. Before this took place we had to speak with a coroner's officer and discuss Daniel's life and what we thought his state of mind had been at the time of his death. The coroner also took a statement from the friend who was with him the night he died. In some instances, such as a suicide, the coroner may wish to speak with other members of the family, to build up a picture of the person prior to the death.

> When Kathy's sister-in-law died, she and her family wrote down their thoughts and observations and what had happened in the weeks before she died. Reading each others' statements was moving and proved to be an insight and a way of sharing how they were all feeling. Although it was hard to do, Kathy found this process very cathartic.

We found the inquest quite an ordeal as it was rather like a court proceeding, with statements being read out. Then the coroner asked questions of us and the friend who had been with Daniel on the night he died. Suddenly, months after the death, we were taken back to the time when it was all fresh and raw. We listened to the details in a public place amongst strangers.

> Becky had to retrace the steps from Jackie's accident to the time of her death some years later.

We went to the inquest as a family and had thought to go and have a coffee in the town afterwards. However we had not realised the emotional impact it would have on us and we just wanted to get home.

> Becky too had not allowed for the effect it would have on her and found that she could not cope at work the following day.

Following the inquest there may be a report in the local paper. This was something we had not been warned about and one of Daniel's friends phoned with a query about what had been written. We had not seen the paper as it was from a different area and none of the family wished to know what it said. It had not occurred to me that it would be reported. I found it very difficult coming to terms with knowing that something so personal to us was now out there in the public domain. How do people cope when, for example, there has been a violent death in the family and they read about it in a national newspaper. It's so easy to be judgemental or critical without knowing the full story or circumstances. Maybe that is why I did not want to read about it: wondering what people would think. Perhaps I could not face just seeing the bare facts.

> When I read reports of suicides, death due to drug overdoses or violence, I want to say, 'remember that is someone's daughter, grandchild, father, wife, uncle. They were once a tiny baby with all the potential and hope that parents dream about. What you read about is such a small part of their lives. You don't know the whole story.'

Sometimes the facts from the inquest are reported wrongly, leading to further distress for the family. Whenever we read of tragedy, we are being faced with someone's loss and pain.

Compensation or insurance claims may have to be dealt with. These may continue for several years – and this too is a continual reminder and 'going over' of the events. There may be many consultations with solicitors. Forms have to be filled in, letters written. Insurance companies may argue against claims made. Daniel had taken out life insurance with his mortgage but the company quibbled over the answer he had given to one of the questions. They argued that he had not been honest. This all hinged on the understanding of the terminology used on the form. Having referred this to several professional people, we came to the conclusion that Daniel's and our understanding was that of the majority of the population but not of the Insurance Company. This kind of situation is all at a time when emotionally, you feel unable to cope with additional stress, and everything is such an effort. It may feel wrong to be arguing over claims for life insurance. The discussion is tossed about in your mind:

'This doesn't feel right.'
'But that's what you pay insurance for.'
'But it's not about the money and it won't bring him back.'
'Well you don't have to claim it.'
'But it's pointless not to claim it; that won't bring him back either. Daniel would have wanted us to have it.'

Receiving money because of Daniel's insurance payments felt very different from inheriting from parents. In that situation, although sadness is still there, you know that an inheritance is from someone making a conscious decision to leave you a gift because they loved you. Insurance claims may involve a tragedy of one kind or another, so then there are very different emotions. We shared Daniel's insurance money with the family. It was difficult to receive it. How can you feel happy when you know you only have it because of tragic, painful circumstances? It is so true that no amount of money will compensate for losing someone you love.

Depending on the circumstances of the death, there may have to be a court case which may take years before it is heard. Until this takes place the relatives of the deceased person may feel very unsettled. It is as if they have been put 'on hold' or like having a black cloud hanging over them.

> This was Becky's experience as she waited for the court case about Jackie's accident. During that time she felt unable to think clearly or make decisions that might affect her future.

There are also many practical issues to be dealt with by the next of kin. Bank accounts may have to be closed or transferred, a house may have to be sold. The local council may have to be notified of

changes in circumstances. Government departments or financial institutions might need to be contacted. These are situations where the extra copies of the death certificate will be useful.

The will needs to be read as soon as possible after the person has died, particularly if there are instructions concerning the funeral. It is the responsibility of the executor/s of the will to ensure that the deceased person's wishes concerning their estate, are carried out. Some people appoint a solicitor as executor but others ask a relative or friend. In that case, probate must be applied for from the local Probate Registry, who will send the appropriate forms. An interview follows when they will talk you through the process and validate the application. You will then be given a certificate of probate which gives the authority to deal with the estate.

Although it is advisable and helpful to have a will, this does not always mean that the person's estate is divided amicably. Sometimes the contents of the will come as a shock to the family and cause bitterness or hurt. Members of the family may choose to contest a will for various reasons. Cases are often reported in the press.

Alternatively one family member may have known that the person had wanted to alter their will but did not have time to do so. Sometimes a will may not have been witnessed and signed correctly, thus making it invalid. Should these wishes be respected? Could the will not be carried out legally and then the family sort it out at a later date to see that the deceased person's wishes were carried out?

> Joan left instructions as to how her estate was to be divided but her will was declared invalid. Two of her intended beneficiaries did not receive anything. This caused upset within her family.

When I hear of rifts in families because of what a will has stated, I always wonder what the person who wrote it would have thought and felt. Did they imagine that their wishes would cause such dissent within their own family?

If there is no will, it would usually be the person's next-of-kin who would apply to the local probate registry for letters of administration which give the authority to dispose of the estate. The question of who inherits in this situation is too involved to discuss here, but there are many myths about who is entitled to what. Advice can be obtained from the Age UK Fact Sheet 14 Dealing with an Estate, Citizens' Advice Bureau or a solicitor.

All these tasks come at a time when the bereaved person's emotional resources are low or non-existent. It is helpful if friends and family are aware of these extra pressures. Help, such as filling in forms or offering transport, may be welcome.

There is one sense in which the funeral is not an ending – because it is the beginning of dealing with all these practical tasks. Many of them will have been put on hold until after the funeral. The bereaved 'responsible relative' is now faced with sorting out paperwork, belongings, finances, property and maybe a host of other things. It may feel like an intrusion into the private life of the person who has died or like a dismantling of their lives. This can be a difficult and upsetting time.

Sometimes dealing with someone's estate can take many months, or even years. Formalities connected to the death may be ongoing during this time. So the bereaved person has a constant reminder of their loved one's death. There may still be more painful feelings to work through, long after everyone around them has 'moved on'. This may prolong their grieving. They may find it difficult to concentrate until everything is finalised. It may hinder them setting out on the journey to find their 'new normality'. Friends and relatives need to be understanding and supportive during this period.

Chapter Six
Belongings

Decisions regarding what to do with a loved one's personal belongings can be a difficult. It may feel as if their possessions are an extension of them, part of who they were. When we dispose of them, either literally or by distributing them amongst family, we may feel we are losing them all over again. It may feel disloyal to get rid of them. It may feel like intruding into their private life and dismantling it bit by bit. It may also bring back painful as well as happy memories.

Following a stroke, my mother came to live with us. She was unable to look after herself and as her mental health deteriorated it became obvious that we could not give her the care she needed. So my mother moved into a Residential Home. She gave me the responsibility of selling her flat and disposing of the contents on her behalf. I found it much harder doing this before she had died than when we did the same for Ian's father, after his death. It felt as if part of her had died before it actually happened, and as if I was making decisions that should have been hers to make. After her death there were just her clothes and a few personal possessions such as photos and ornaments left. In some ways they were harder to deal with than furniture and tableware. For many years she had worn pleated skirts, and jumpers which she had knitted herself. To me, they were so much part of who she was. For several years I left the jumpers in a box in the loft. I could not cope with getting rid of them, yet I did not want them myself. Eventually I gave them to a charity, but put them in a bag to be taken away, rather than give them to a local shop. That avoided the possibility of seeing someone wearing the clothes in question, which may have been distressing.

Rob took his wife's clothes to a local charity shop, and was quite shaken when he later saw one of the items in the shop window.

Eleven years on I still have a box of items from my mother's kitchen that periodically I take out, look at and then put back. They are not things from my mother's later life, but rather from my childhood. I don't wish to use them and I have no room for them in my kitchen and yet for some reason I hold on to them. Even after all this time, this box still feels like an obstacle to contend with.

Fran kept some tablecloths that had belonged to her mother. She did not want to use them but felt unable to get rid of them until some years later. She was getting ready to move house and felt able to part with them then.

Often our emotions and logic do not seem to fit comfortably together. Deciding on a sensible course of action will not necessarily take unexpected emotions into account.

It may be worth noting here that if the deceased has been 'in care,' their belongings will generally have to be removed quickly. So it may be helpful if they can be kept somewhere temporarily so that decisions do not have to be made in a hurry.

Daniel had lived by himself in his own house, and when he died we had to clear his house so it could be sold. At the time our family was obviously in a state of shock and distress. I could not even cope with going to his home, so it was left to Ian and our other sons to deal with his belongings. If we had to go through a similar experience again, I think I would ask to do it differently. I would not want to do everything in such a rush. With hindsight, it would have been so helpful if someone had come along and said:

'Don't get rid of his personal things until you've had time to think more about what you would and would not like to keep.'

Even though I had the experience of keeping some of my

mother's belongings, I was unable to draw on that experience for this situation. Decisions were made 'on the spot'.

> One of our boys brought Daniel's roller boots home. Several years earlier, when Dan had been living at home, he used to go to work on them. Seeing them so unexpectedly was something I could not cope with at that moment in time. They were so much a part of his quirky character. So I just threw them in the dustbin, which was emptied the following morning.

How I wished I had put them in a box in the garage where I would not have been able to see them but I could then have made a rational decision at a later date. They were so much a part of him that I wish I had kept them.

> Ann hadn't been able to go through the things Harry had left behind. Most of them were all packed up since he had moved out of the house.
>
> Sally could not face seeing her baby's clothes at the time of his death, but later wished she had kept some of them.

It is good to give ourselves time, before making decisions which involve such painful emotions and memories.

> Becky felt pressured by a counsellor to clear out Jackie's bedroom shortly after her death. She had already disposed of the clothes

she had worn while in hospital and rehabilitation. But she was not yet ready to deal with her bedroom.

Sometimes when a child has died, parents leave the bedroom as it was at the time of death, for many years or for always. There are those who would say that is an unhealthy attitude, but how are we to know? When should we let go of tangible reminders? When should we get rid of the clothes hanging in the wardrobe? Maybe if we are trapped by these things and they stop us from getting on with our lives, we need professional help to come to terms with what has happened.

> We still have Daniel's only suit in a wardrobe. He was so proud when he bought it to be best man at his friend's wedding. Perhaps it is a reminder of what seemed like an achievement for him.

Sometimes friends or relatives may feel they are being helpful by removing things that belonged to the deceased person.

> Helen's relatives moved her husband's coat from the back door where it had always hung. They thought it would upset her to see it all the time. Helen put it back. The sight of his coat was not going to add to the pain she felt at his loss. She needed it there.

Particularly in the early days, the feeling of loss seems to take over your whole being. It may be comforting to see things that belonged to our loved one, or it may be overwhelmingly painful. However it is not up to other people to decide what is good for us to keep, or to dispose of. We need to do that ourselves, when the time is right.

Some people have photos, and other items belonging to the deceased person in their home. Others may have none at all. We have photos of Daniel at various stages in his life and a few of his things around the house. Some of them remind us of the time he spent working in the brewery, which was probably the happiest time in his life. However when a friend recently asked if I would like to see a video she had of Daniel when he was a young boy, I felt I couldn't cope with that. Maybe I needed time to prepare myself emotionally because that felt as if I would suddenly be 'seeing him in the flesh'. One day I may ask to see it.

We have a chest containing some of Daniel's belongings and from time to time I take them out and look at them. Sometimes it is a comfort seeing all these things and at other times it causes distress; such a mixture of emotions. One of our sons was still single when Daniel died, and so his wife had never met him. One evening they looked through the chest together, which helped her form a clearer picture of who he was. It helped her to be able to think of him as a real person.

So we can see that tangible reminders of our loved ones may be helpful to some people, but not to others. We can't decide what is right for someone else. However, the memories we have, cannot be taken or given away. They will always be there in our hearts and minds: always included in our family history up until that point when they died.

Chapter Seven
Beginning the Journey

So what is it like as we begin this unknown journey? What are those first few weeks and months like?

For me it was as if life as I knew it had stopped. I could not take in what had happened. Surely it was a nightmare from which I would wake? I remember feeling as if I was 'somewhere else'. Nothing felt real. I certainly wasn't functioning how I usually did. Some of the time I was just sitting, staring into space, or going around like a zombie doing things automatically. Other times, I would keep crying. This went on for many months. There was a definite sense of unreality. How could Daniel have died when I had seen him a few days before, and he had been fit and well? I wanted to be able to ask him what had happened that night. He had been so looking forward to starting a new job. Each day came and went in a blur, even while Ian and I were trying to organise the funeral and deal with all the formalities.

How precious our friends and family were at that time. One of them took us to the mortuary to identify Daniel's body and see him for one last time. Others came with grocery shopping and ready-cooked meals. Still others came with flowers; to say, 'I'm sorry'; to give a comforting hug. We were so fortunate to be surrounded by friends who gave us their love and support. It felt like being wrapped in a cocoon. It was as if my world had shrunk to our home and anyone who came into it. The outside world ceased to exist.

Much has been written about the stages of grief. Some of these will be there at the beginning. Others will come later. Still others may not be experienced at all. There is no right order or time limit to them but we try to deal with them as they arise. We may feel we have dealt with certain issues, only to find they raise their heads again at a later time. They include a whole range of emotions and thoughts which we will consider briefly here.

Disbelief is a likely response when someone has died suddenly.

'How can he be dead when I waved him goodbye this morning?'

'He was fit and well when I last saw him.'

Even when someone has been ill for a long time there may that sense of:

'I still can't believe he's gone.'

Some people find it hard to accept the death when they have not seen the body. There is no evidence that the person has died. It's just what they've been told.

Doreen's son died abroad where he had lived for several years. It was difficult for her to grasp the reality of it.

There may be a feeling of longing: a yearning to see them again; to touch them; to hold them; to hear their voice that one more time. We may hardly recognise this feeling as we come home to an empty house and call out 'I'm back!.' We lay the dinner table for three, when there's now only two.

Sometimes there are feelings of guilt. What if? Why didn't I?

We wonder if it was our fault. Could I have done more? If only . . .
Often, these questions arise from our fragile emotional state, and
when we can think logically, we will think differently. However, if
there are areas where our guilt is justified, we may need help in
coming to terms with these.

We may experience feelings of anger. Sometimes this may
seem justified. The widow whose husband has left her with huge
debts. The mother who now has to bring up the children on her
own and look for a job to cope financially. Anger may be mixed
up with resentment at having been left to cope with the situation.
In other instances the anger may not seem logical and will take
you by surprise. After a long illness, the question may be asked,
'Why did he go and leave me now?' as though the person had
died on purpose.

> One of Daniel's friends and I initially felt angry with him, even
> though we didn't know the facts surrounding his death. I wanted
> to shout at him, 'What did you think you were doing? How could
> you be so stupid?'

Surely such questions come out of our hurt, bewilderment and
grief?

How does the young mother with several children manage when
her husband dies? She needs to find space and time to grieve, but
she has to continue with the daily task of looking after her family.
How does she help her children through *their* grief while trying to
cope with her own? It is so helpful if she has family or friends who
can take over now and again to give her that much-needed time.
What about parents whose young child has died? They may have
other children who are still quite young and they will need their
parents' support and comfort even while they are trying to cope
with their own grief.

After her mother died, Sarah said:

> 'I haven't got time to grieve, there's too much to do with the
> children. There's no space.'

Although grieving is a very individual emotional journey, it is helpful to be able to share grief with family or friends. When my father died, in his late fifties, we children were all living in different places. We went our separate ways after the funeral. With hindsight I can see that we missed out on the 'togetherness' of grieving. Although I think I supported my mother as best as I could, I do not feel we supported each other as siblings. I know that I felt out of my depth in that situation. There was the shock of what had happened and trying to manage my own feelings.

Years later, Marjorie, about the same age as my mother, told me:

'My husband died in his fifties and my children and I just grieved on our own. We didn't share our feelings. You didn't in those days. We didn't grieve together'

It would be good to think that attitudes toward grieving have changed in the intervening years, and that we are more aware of the effects death can have. There is more support and advice available now. Sharing grief helps to ease the burden.

When Daniel died we wanted to be able to grieve together as a family. I don't know how well we did in those early days. I've always thought that it's acceptable for children to see their parents upset, as that is part of life. Yet I didn't want to cry in front of my grown-up children, because I felt it was hard enough for them to cope with their own grief. I didn't want them to feel that they had to support their mother as well. However, crying in front of your children, whether adult or young, lets them know that it's a good and healthy reaction. Maybe it gives them permission to cry as well: part of the grieving together.

'One of our boys was still living at home and I would often say to him, 'I'm having a rubbish day today.' There were shared hugs or gentle touches.'

Being able to cry is a good release for all the pent-up emotions.

I have heard people say that they are afraid to let go and cry in case they never stop. I have never heard of that happening.

> Lillian kept very busy after her husband died following a short illness. Several weeks later she suddenly found herself sobbing for about two hours. Later she told a friend, who said, 'Is that the first real good cry you've had?' When she confirmed that it was, the friend said, 'Well, I expect it did you good.' Lillian agreed.

When someone has been very ill for a long time prior to the death, there may be differing emotions to deal with. Some people think that because the suffering is over, it somehow lessens the grieving. Susan experienced that:

> 'A friend of mine who lived in the village and had been quite involved with Joanne's last couple of months – the end of life stage – said, 'well, you must be feeling better now'.
> I replied, 'no, I've gone from one nightmare to another'.'

In the case of someone with dementia, it may be that some of the grieving has already taken place. I remember feeling that I was losing my mother bit by bit, as the person she used to be disappeared. When a loved one no longer recognises you and is unable to communicate with you, there is a feeling almost that they have died already. Similarly, the grieving process may also have begun when someone has been seriously ill.

> Carol commented that she had not cried since her sister died, and wondered if she would do later. She thought it might be because she had watched her 'slipping away' for such a long time. Had she done her grieving day by day and week by week?

Yet until that moment of death, the final parting has not occurred, so the emotional impact of that may be the same, whatever the circumstances.

When someone has a terminal illness, there is the opportunity to voice all the things that friends and family might wish to say to each other. There is time for everyone to 'put their house in order' in practical and emotional terms. Relationships may be healed during this time. There is an opportunity to part with no regrets at things unsaid or left undone. There is time for what might be called a 'good ending'.

However, in the case of a sudden death, those who are left behind may have to deal with much that is unfinished. They may have to come to terms with the angry words, a broken relationship, the unfinished conversations. There will be additional emotional turmoil as they try to work through these issues. Common to all is knowing that there was no opportunity to say 'goodbye'.

When a loved one has been ill for a long time, there may be a sense of relief when they die. We are glad that their pain and suffering has ended. But this may be followed by feelings of guilt. Will people think I am glad they have died? It is very upsetting and stressful to watch someone we love struggle and cope with what may have been an horrendous illness. There is a sense in which we have suffered too, so might the sense of relief be for ourselves as well?

> In the last year or two of my mother's life, we were told several times that she might not live through the night. Then, in the morning, she would be sitting up in bed eating her breakfast, and the staff would always be so pleased. 'Your mother's rallied round. Isn't that good?'

For me it was an emotional roller-coaster: one part of me not wanting her to die, but the other not wanting her to be in such a fragile mental and physical state. Dementia is like a living death, and hard for relatives and friends to cope with.

Whatever the circumstances surrounding the death, there is such a mixture of emotions. Our emotional responses will not be the same as those of anyone else: they are unique to us. No-one can know how we feel. Our relationship with the deceased person is also unlike that of anyone else. So we begin this unknown journey into uncharted territory.

Break, Break, Break

Break, break, break,
    On thy cold grey stones, O sea!
And I would that my tongue could utter
    The thoughts that arise in me.

O, well for the fisherman's boy,
    That he shouts with his sister at play!
O, well for the sailor lad,
    That he sings in his boat on the bay!

And the stately ships go on
    To their haven under the hill;
But O for the touch of a vanished hand,
    And the sound of a voice that is still!

Break, break, break,
    At the foot of thy crags, O sea!
But the tender grace of a day that is dead
    Will never come back to me.

(Lord Tennyson)

Chapter Eight
Early Days

In those early days, Daniel's death and everything associated with it, was there in the forefront of my mind. It overshadowed everything. The grief felt overwhelming. I couldn't imagine ever laughing again. How could I, when my son was dead?

> At night, a longing for sleep that would not come. Instead, the release of tears: a sense of despair.
> In the morning, a longing to hide from the world: not wanting to get up and face the day ahead.

This may sound like someone who is depressed, and there are many similarities. This is part of the terrain that takes some people by surprise. You feel exhausted and yet you can't sleep. There may a lack of motivation to do even the things you used to enjoy.

> After their brother died, Michael and Neil found that their memory and concentration were badly affected. This consequently impacted on their work.

I think it was probably after the funeral that I began to very slowly emerge from this cocooned and dream-like existence. There comes a time when we have to try to become part of the world around us again. We have to find a way of living without the person who has died.

I remember the first time I went out on my own after Daniel's death. It was a situation I was anxious about. I decided to go to the local supermarket to get that 'first time' over. On the way I met an elderly couple I knew. I explained to them what I was doing and they kindly offered to come with me. However it was something I felt I needed to do by myself. I had decided that if I saw anyone I knew, I would approach them, and say 'hello' and chat with them. Hopefully, they would then know that talking with me did not have to be difficult or awkward. I wanted to do this after hearing, so many times, of people crossing over to the other side of the road to avoid speaking to someone bereaved. I felt it would be good to follow Elsie's example after her husband died:

> 'I felt that she was walking down the other side of the street because she didn't know what to say. So I crossed the road, thinking 'this is going to be hard,' and just started a conversation with her. I think she was relieved.'

As I walked up the road I wondered what people would think when they saw me. Would they be embarrassed? Would they look at me with pity in their eyes? There was a rumour going round the town that Daniel had committed suicide. Would they be making judgements on Daniel and us? How would I cope with questions about his death – questions to which I didn't know the answers? Maybe I wouldn't want to tell them even if I knew. Would I burst into tears in the middle of the supermarket? The thought of how it might be was actually worse than the reality. I didn't experience any of the things I had dreaded, and as time went on it became easier to deal with the unexpected questions or reactions of others.

How do we know if we are ready to face the world again? We all react and cope differently. After my mother died I felt I needed to keep busy, but after Daniel died I wanted to be quiet and still. I spent hours in the garden, and it was several months before I started doing some of the voluntary work I had been involved in before. I was able to resume this on the understanding that I could just go home if I felt unable to cope. However, I felt unable to return to the part-time job I had with vulnerable young people with physical disabilities. I wasn't sure that I would be able to 'hold myself together'. It wasn't a job that I could just leave and go home, as we were often working in a one-to-one situation. Ian went back to his job as a GP surgery counsellor and church minister just a few weeks later. Some people, including me, thought it was too soon, given the nature of his work. However we are all different. We have to work out what is best for us, regardless of what other people may think.

> Peggy returned to work very shortly after the death of her son, as she felt she needed the support of her colleagues. Maybe the routine also gave her a sense of normality and a focus.
>
> Becky said, 'What will I do all day if I don't go back to work? I'll just sit and mope.'

One experience that appears to be common to many bereaved people, is noticing that life goes on for others as though nothing out-of-the-ordinary has happened. We can feel hurt that our friends and colleagues seem to forget so soon that we are still grieving. There is almost an expectation that we will be 'back to normal' after a few weeks, if not sooner.

> I started receiving phone calls from work about a week after Daniel died, wanting to know when I was going back. I found it difficult to cope with that pressure.
>
> At a family wedding shortly after the death of his daughter, Jeff was asked what was the matter with him as he wasn't the 'life and soul of the party'.

> A few months after Daniel died I met a friend who greeted me with, 'Hello, how are you?.' When I replied, 'So-so,' she responded with 'Why, what's the matter?.'

I have heard the early days of grief likened to walking through a dark tunnel. However, even in those early days, there were times when I caught a glimpse of a light at the end of it. The five minutes of being able to focus on other things would sometimes lengthen to half-an-hour. Gradually that rawness of grief subsided. Very slowly there was just a taste of the new normality that was to come.

Sometimes people say that they feel guilty when they realise that they have gone a whole morning or day without thinking of the deceased person. It feels wrong, or disrespectful, to laugh and have a good time. Somehow it feel as if they are forgetting the person who has died. Yet we need to work our way towards finding purpose in life again. It will not be the same as before. The focus of our day-to-day living may change. We may find we need a different direction to our life. But it is possible for life to become meaningful and enjoyable again.

The dreams we have in the night often become vague and muddled by the morning but, sometimes, bits come back with vivid clarity. Those early days after Daniel's death have become like that. Much is a blur in my memory. The events and the feelings have mostly faded. However. there are still occasions when I can be transported back to those weeks and months. There are reminders: maybe a song, a question asked, a place visited. Then the unreality and the longing for it to be just a dream, rise to the surface again. Even now, eleven years later, I can momentarily feel that intensity of grief that was there at the beginning. But I feel stronger now, and know that I have found a comfortable place within myself for Daniel to rest.

Chapter Nine
Responding to the Bereaved

So how should people react or respond when they are faced with someone who has been bereaved by the death of a close friend or relative?

I have already written about the practical help and visits we received in the early days following Daniel's death. For many people there will be family staying; friends calling in; flowers and cards arriving. But what about the weeks and months that follow?

Over the years I have heard so many stories. These have been from the extremes of friends coming to tell you what you ought to do, to friends crossing over the road to avoid having to converse with you, or people talking to you as though nothing had happened. However, many people feel they do not know what to say to someone who has been bereaved. This may be more so if the death is, for instance, the result of suicide; a drug-related or violent incident; or the death of a child. They may be anxious about saying the wrong thing. Perhaps they think they will cause more distress if they mention the death. Some people cannot cope being with someone in distress: it makes them feel uncomfortable or helpless. Sometimes people make tactless comments, which may be difficult to handle at the time, but usually they are doing their best to offer comfort. We have probably all had times when we've said something and then thought, 'why did I say that?' or 'that came out all wrong'.

Sometimes what is said in fun can touch a raw spot in someone else.

A group of women were discussing in a light-hearted way how annoying it was that their husbands snore. Then one lady said that that she would give anything to hear her husband snoring, as her husband had died the previous year.

So how should we respond to someone who has been bereaved? We may be afraid of saying the wrong thing. Is it best to take a risk and say *something* so that at least the death has been acknowledged? Should we not say anything, and maybe cause hurt, because the bereaved person thinks we don't care? I think it is best to err on the side of saying something, even if it is just 'I'm sorry to hear about . . .' A hug, if appropriate, also shows that we care.

I think there is a sense in which whatever we say may cause upset, depending on how the bereaved person is feeling at the time. Their emotions will be 'all over the place' for quite a while. They may react to what we say, in a way that seems out of character with how we know them. So we need to be able to put our own feelings aside as we offer our support on this journey they are setting out on.

However, there are some things that we should avoid saying and I will just mention some that I have heard many times.

'Never mind, you can always have another one,' is sometimes

said to couples who have lost a baby during pregnancy. This shows insensitivity and a lack of understanding of their loss. It may be helpful to show extra care around the time when the baby would have been born. The death of an unborn child may cause other difficulties. Sometimes the pregnancy has not been announced and so that makes it harder to talk about it. In the case of an induced abortion, when there may be secrecy, guilt or shame attached to it, this can prevent the death even being acknowledged, and so there is little, if any, sharing of grief.

'At least you've still got the others' may be said when a child has died. Having other children can never make up for the one that has died. It may feel as if the person is implying that the one who has died didn't matter because you still have the others.

'Time is a great healer' is a common phrase that is used. This is not helpful. I have lost track of the number of grieving people who have said, 'You never get over it, you just learn how to cope with it better.' 'You learn to live with it.'

Time, of itself, does not heal. We need to find that healing within us, however long it takes. Some people never seem to find that inner place of peace, however much time has elapsed.

'Well, at least you didn't have to watch him suffer,' is sometimes said after an unexpected death, such as from a heart attack. That statement may be true, but there has been no warning, and no preparation. The shock of it adds to the emotional turmoil. There will have been no time to say 'goodbye'; 'I love you'; 'sorry'; or anything else that may leave regrets. So if this thought is to be spoken, it needs to be at the right time by the right person.

Sensitivity is always needed when talking to someone who has been bereaved, especially if we do not know them very well.

One Sunday when Ian was leading a church service he mentioned the fact that our eldest son had died. Afterwards, the lady sitting next to me wanted to know what he had died from. Even though I told her that I would rather not talk about it, she kept persisting.

Other than with very close friends, I was not able to talk about the cause of Daniel's death for about two years. That was a big obstacle on my path for me to contend with. However, it did not pose a problem for other members of our family. We need to respect other people's feelings.

However, if people are not told the facts then they may make up their own version of what happened. This was brought home to me, on two separate occasions, several years after Daniel's death. These two conversations probably caused more upset to the people who were talking to me, than they did to me.

> 'I've really struggled with suicidal feelings . . . You know all about that because of Daniel . . . Oh, I'm sorry, I thought he committed suicide.'

> 'Of course some people bring about their own death because of their life-style, like Daniel . . . Oh, I'm sorry, I thought he was on drugs.'

Sometimes our offers of help can be made in the wrong way. Friends who say, 'give me a ring if there is anything I can do,' may be disappointed if their offer is not taken up. However, the grieving person may not feel able to pick up the phone and ask. There is often an inability to ask for help, especially in the early days. It may be more helpful to be specific. 'Would you like me to do your shopping this week?' The same could apply if suggesting they might like to call round sometime for a cup of tea. 'Would you like to come for a cup of tea on Wednesday afternoon?' Be mindful that socialising of any kind may be difficult for a while.

> Shortly after Daniel died, Julia invited me out to coffee. She wanted to take me 'somewhere nice'. I couldn't even cope with the thought of it. Fortunately I was able to explain how I felt and she asked what I would like to do instead. Being able to go to her home, knowing I could 'be myself' and talk about Daniel if I wanted to, was what I appreciated at that time.

Friends sometimes suggest going away for a holiday straight

after the death; and for some, that may be a helpful thing to do. They may appreciate a complete change. It may help them adjust. However, others go away because they cannot cope with all the memories in their home.

> 'We just didn't want to be at home with all the memories of our daughter there.'

Others, like Ian and me, may initially feel a need to be at home all the time. Maybe home becomes a safe place, and provides security for a while.

> 'When I'm out, I just want to get home as quickly as I can.'

Those who find themselves on their own following a death, may find going away difficult for a different reason:

> 'I can't cope with coming home to an empty house.'

I heard of one couple who have never been on holiday since their daughter died many years ago. Their home is still as it was when she died. Perhaps they feel unable to leave those tangible reminders.

So home can be our refuge or a reminder of all the sadness. We all have our own ways of coping.

Some people will suggest that keeping busy is the best way of dealing with bereavement. Usually this is because they think it will 'take your mind off it'. In the very early days, the likelihood of that is remote, but later on it is helpful to have times of 'doing normal things' as well as time to grieve. This is sometimes referred to as a 'moving in and out of the grieving process'. We need to grieve but we also need to take time off from it. I found as the months went by, the time spent grieving lessened, and the time spent 'living life again' increased.

Should we just 'drop in' on someone who has recently been bereaved? This is a sensitive issue and it may depend on how well we know the person, and on the person themselves.

David felt very strongly about people calling in to see him after his wife had died.

> 'And don't just go round and bang on the door unless you know them very well indeed. Phone and say "Is it alright for me to come round?" It's far better.'

Yet I really appreciated the friend who knocked on the door and said, 'Can I come in and ask you how you are?.'

Being aware of the family situation is also important. There may have been unresolved conflict within the family, with the one who has died. If there has been an acrimonious divorce it may be difficult for children when a parent dies. Sometimes the one who has died has been estranged from the family, who may then be faced with feelings of guilt or regret. Extra sensitivity will be called for, where there are such issues.

It is important to remember that everyone's journey with grief is different. Some people will want to talk about it all the time, while for others it will be very private. However, we shouldn't be afraid of bringing the deceased person into the conversation when it feels natural to do so.

> 'Harry would have loved to have come on this outing with us.'

> 'Billy would have been twenty-one today wouldn't he?'

This lets the bereaved person know we feel comfortable talking about their loved one. It's a way of giving them permission to talk as well if they wish.

I hope all this hasn't seemed too daunting. Be open to being, saying or doing what is needed at that particular moment. It may be, 'Let me do your washing.' It may be sitting in silence. Respond in a way that shows you care and are available if they want company along the way. Friends and family can do much to help in the healing of bereavement.

I think Susan summed it up when she said:

'You just want someone to listen while you say what if feels like.
I think that what you desperately yearn for, are people who will walk the path with you.'

Chapter Ten
Feelings Within

We have considered how to respond to those who have been bereaved. I thought it might be helpful to look briefly at our reactions and feelings towards people and situations when we have been bereaved ourselves.

Particularly in the early days, we feel very vulnerable and sensitive. Our emotions are all over the place, and often we feel we have no control over them. Patience may be in short supply. We may feel irritable, and generally more intolerant than usual. Grief affects us all differently, and often in ways that surprise us. I remember a friend saying to me,

'No-one told me it would be like this.'

A few days after Daniel died, a friend, who knew Daniel and about his difficulties in coping, said to me,

'Well, you won't have to worry about him anymore.'

I knew that she meant it as a means of comfort. As a statement of fact, it was right, but I didn't want his death to be the reason for not worrying about him any more. That would never compensate for him dying. My emotions could not cope with hearing that then. Knowing that I did not have to worry about him any more did not seem to be of any relevance when faced with his death. Yet Ian and I have said the same thing to each other since then, and it is of some comfort now. We often used to ask each other what would happen to Daniel when we died? He would probably have continued to need support; and although his brothers were very caring of him, they might not always have been in a position to be there when he needed them.

In a similar way, a grieving widower may know that his wife will not suffer any more pain after a life-threatening illness, but that doesn't stop him wishing she was still with him.

Our 'heads' and our 'hearts' do not always sit comfortably together.

Sometimes we can surprise ourselves by our reactions to others.

I remember meeting a lady I had known for a very short time as a work colleague. She asked how Daniel was getting on and I told her he had died. There were the usual condolences and then she gave me an invitation to visit her if I needed someone to talk to. I know that my response to her offer was not very gracious. I did not want to 'open my heart' to her. I did not know her well enough and yet I knew that she was being kind. I didn't know how to reply without appearing ungrateful.

I found I was unable to do some of the things I used to do, such as meeting with friends. One of them couldn't understand why things had changed; and I couldn't really explain it to myself, let alone to her. I found myself saying, in quite an abrupt and uncharacteristic way, something like, 'Well, that's how it is, so you'll just have to deal with it.'

I did find it hard when people I did not know very well wanted to talk about Daniel and how I was coping. This could be face-to-face, or on the phone. They were mostly people connected to our local area church denomination. I felt that they were intruding into my private space. I wanted to tell them that it was nothing to do with them as I didn't really know them and why should I want to share something so personal with them? It was a pressure I didn't need, made worse by knowing that they were trying to show their love and concern.

It was when having to deal with these sort of situations that I felt that the path I was walking seemed rough and steep. I did not always feel that I had the emotional energy to tackle it.

Another situation that can be difficult to cope with, is when people 'grade' the effect they think a death has had on someone, as Harriet experienced when her sister died:

> 'Somehow they thought it wasn't as bad for me, being her sister, as it was for my parents.'

Similarly, Rebecca found that people asked her how her husband, Neil, was, after the death of his brother, but didn't seem interested in how she was. This was hard, as Rebecca had quite a special relationship with her brother-in-law.

> 'It was as if because I was only a sister-in-law, my grief was less, and therefore I couldn't be suffering as much.'

These attitudes are an added burden, at a time when we need support and understanding. Other people can't know the depth of someone's grief.

> After her father died, his best friend took to his bed for two days.

> One of Daniel's neighbours needed to take time off work.

It is interesting that compassionate leave from the workplace is often only for close relatives, which seems to reinforce the idea of grief being graded in people's minds. Yet we may feel as devastated following the death of a very close friend as we do after an elderly parent has died.

Another situation that I found difficult to cope with as the bereaved person, was meeting people in the street and not knowing if they had heard about Daniel's death. These would be people I knew well enough to stop and have a chat with, but who were not close friends. If they asked how the family were, then I had an opportunity to tell them. If it became obvious from the conversation that they did not know, and there was no opening, then I would have to decide whether to tell them. How do you just drop into the conversation that your son has died? Would I be able to cope with their reaction? Would I get too upset? Usually I did tell them. Sometimes they would be embarrassed and full of apologies because they did not know. Others were able to say simply and sincerely, 'I'm so sorry.' At other times I was aware that people did not know what to say. Would it have been better not to tell them? If I kept quiet and they found out later, they might feel awkward the next time I met them.

Answering the questions about the cause of his death was the hardest. In the days before we knew, it was probably more awkward for the person who had asked, as usually you know why someone has died. What could they say when I replied, 'I don't know'? Once we did know, as I have already said, it was a long time before I felt comfortable in answering the question about how he died.

Sometimes when somebody is going through a difficulty or tragedy, friends will say, 'I know just how you feel.' It's an expression that we use quite lightly and we know it's meant as a way of showing empathy. But actually, no-one knows how we are feeling about anything. When someone said it to me, I can remember feeling quite angry. How could they possibly know? I wanted to shout at them, 'No, you don't! You have no idea how I feel.'

Since Daniel died, I have met several other people whose sons have died. Yes, I have some understanding of what they are going through but I would never claim to know how they are feeling.

We are all different and unique, and because of this we will react to circumstances in varying ways even when life is going well for us. I hope this chapter will have given some insight into a few of the added issues that we bereaved people have to deal with at a time when our emotional strength is low. Sometimes it is all we can do to cope with ourselves, and get through to the next day, without having to interact with anyone else. So make allowances for out-of-character behaviour or sharp retorts. Don't be offended if you get what seems like an ungrateful response. We may be having a really bad day. The clouds may not yet have given way to sunshine. The path may still seem very rough and steep.

Chapter Eleven
Along the Journey

Everyone's experiences of bereavement are different. The ways in which we handle our grief will vary, as there is no right or wrong way. Much of our coming to terms with what has happened, and our healing, will take place within the warmth and love of our family and friends.

But what are some of these ways in which bereavement affects the lives of those who grieve?

Maybe Susan summed it up when she said that,

> 'You've experienced something that changes you for ever and causes you to re-examine your life: and I say that every single bit of your life is touched – no bit is untouched.'

Andrew felt that,

> 'You are never going to return to that previous place as normality – it's a different landscape.'

We have to adjust to a new reality, some parts of which may be temporary but some may be permanent.

For the first few months I felt that I was 'somewhere else'. Life was going on all around me, yet I did not feel a part of it. I have heard other bereaved people make similar comments.

> 'There is a sense that everything and everyone is moving around me, while I stand still with empty arms that long to hold my son.'

For an even longer time I had what I would call 'really bad days'. Initially I tried to 'fight them' but eventually realised that they were just part of my journey. So I would have my bad day and not worry about it. Tomorrow was a new day to start again.

Suddenly all the things you take for granted, and your security in knowing who you are and what you are doing, are taken away. You have to look for this new normal, and yet it is too soon, as you struggle with the hurt, sadness – and maybe anger – at what has happened. For the people around you, life continues as it always has. Unless they have had experience of grief, in themselves or someone else, they will often assume that you have 'got over it' as your life takes on a semblance of normality again.

I have sometimes heard people say that they felt very vulnerable after someone close to them had died. There seems to be a heightened sensitivity, and an inability to cope with situations which would not have caused a problem before. Even a simple thing like going shopping can cause anxiety. Ordinary everyday activities sometimes become an ordeal for a while. There may be a lack of motivation to do even the small things.

> 'I can't see the point of doing housework any more when there's nobody here to see it.'

> 'I'd rather stay in bed so that I don't have to face the world.'

> 'I can't be bothered to phone my friends.'

Even having to make simple choices can feel overwhelming.

> Elizabeth found she could not cope with shopping. Panic would set in. There were too many grocery items to choose from or the required item was not on the shelf. On one occasion in the middle of doing her shopping she just left the partly-full shopping trolley in the aisle, and went home.

In a previous chapter I mentioned the differing feelings we can have towards home. It may be our sanctuary, so that we find it difficult to go out. Alternatively it may be a place of sad memories to be avoided, so it becomes easier to keep going out or away on holiday.

Sometimes it may be hard to go back home to an empty house, even after only an hour or so away. No-one to greet you; no-one to talk to; no-one to know that you've come home and you're safe.

> 'I'd taken the boys for tea at a friend's house. When we got home I rang her and said, "I got back safely," and I could almost hear her on the end of the phone thinking, "What's she on about, what's she ringing me for?"

> 'I often find myself calling out "I'm back," forgetting that there's no-one there to hear.'

> 'I always phone my friend when I get home or nobody will know I'm still alive.'

Relationships may change, or friendships even end, following bereavement.

> 'You find out who your friends are . . . I remember thinking about all the friendships . . . and actually, how easy it is not to be a part of that and how easy they let you go.'

This is probably due to people not knowing what to say or do in the circumstances, rather than making a deliberate choice to end the friendship. Then time passes and relationships drift apart. Alternatively, the person themselves may withdraw from any social contact because they cannot cope with it at the time. Friends may not understand and so they stop trying to keep in touch. It is so easy for bereaved people to become socially isolated.

Soon after Daniel died, a friend warned me that we may find all the 'firsts' difficult. The first anniversary of the death. The first birthday or wedding anniversary without them. The first

Christmas. The first holiday as a single person for someone who has been part of a couple for many years. The first family get-together with one person missing. The 'firsts' will vary according to the situation.

Susan remembered:

> 'All those firsts; Mother's Day without a card, your birthday, their birthday. Through that year they all bring different challenges.'

Even after many years when you may feel that you have 'got your feelings under control, something may remind you of your loss.

As Susan continued:

> 'Sometimes you're prepared for something and you psyche yourself up – and you can kind of deal with it – and other times it catches you sideways.'

Suddenly you can be back in that painful place. Another friend likened it to 'being ambushed' by your emotions.

> Elsie was on holiday and found herself in a situation that suddenly reminded her of her husband's death about thirty years previously. She hadn't been thinking about him, but there it was in her thoughts. Ambushed!

> Ian, watching *Downton Abbey* on the television heard a comment about 'my firstborn son'. Even though it was not an expression he would have used himself, he was suddenly taken back to the birth of our firstborn son, Daniel. Ambushed!

For me, these kind of incidents represent the hidden dangers of my journey. They are the ones that I can't see or prepare for.

It may be little things that trigger these emotions: hearing a favourite song, seeing someone wearing the same clothes, doing an activity they would have loved.

Even eleven years later, my heart still does a slight lurch whenever I see someone riding a mountain bike, wearing a black cap. Seeing them from behind, it could be Daniel. Ambushed!

Sometimes, certain places can bring back painful memories.

A few days after Daniel died I asked a friend to take me for a walk by a nearby river. It was a long time before I could go there again because of the association with the awful distress I felt then.

Hazel couldn't cope going into church, hearing all the singing, as it conjured up pictures of her husband enjoying the worship in church. It was too painful.

For a long time, Phyllis felt unable to go to friends' funerals at the church where her husband's funeral had been held.

The length of time between these reminders and the death do not seem to relate to the depth of upset. Even after many years the grief can suddenly be there again, and you may feel disorientated by it for a while.

All these things are part of our grieving journey. Sometimes it feels like a smooth ride and other times, a bumpy one.

When Ian and I go on a long car journey we have several stops, so that we don't get too tired. So it is with grieving. At times we can feel exhausted from it and so we need to have breaks. We need to sit and rest, before resuming the journey.

I remember walking along a coastal path with a friend. We came to a place where we were not sure which path to take. We made our choice and carried on for some considerable distance, uphill and through overgrown patches. We thought we were making progress, until we suddenly realised we were back at our starting point. There are times when grieving feels like that. We think that we are managing well, coping with the tricky bits, apparently making progress, and suddenly it feels like we are back at the beginning. So we pick ourselves up and continue on our way.

Soon after Daniel died a friend said to me,

'At the moment it feels like there's a jagged stone inside you that is turning round and round causing great pain. In time the jagged rough parts will become smooth. The stone will still be there, but it won't hurt as much.'

Eleven years later on, I can agree with her: the stone has become smooth and the journey does not seem so rough as at first.

Time Does Not Bring Relief: You All Have Lied

Time does not bring relief; you all have lied
Who told me time would ease me of my pain!
I miss him in the weeping of the rain;
I want him at the shrinking of the tide;
The old snows melt from every mountain-side,
And last year's leaves are smoke in every lane;
But last year's bitter loving must remain
Heaped on my heart, and my old thoughts abide.
There are a hundred places where I fear
To go,—so with his memory they brim.
And entering with relief some quiet place
Where never fell his foot or shone his face
I say, 'There is no memory of him here!'
And so stand stricken, so remembering him.

(Edna St Vincent Millay)

Chapter Twelve
Changes

When a baby is born, new relationships and roles are created. Husbands and wives, or partners, become fathers and mothers. Their siblings become aunts and uncles. Their parents become grandparents. An only child now has a brother or sister, so they are now the eldest child.

It is similar when someone dies. The whole dynamics of the family are changed, and roles within in it may alter. Everyone will find themselves in a different position within the family structure.

When parents die in old age, their children no longer have that older person there for advice or to share things with. It may be the first time that they have had no-one older in the family to turn to in a time of need. Suddenly they find themselves in the position of being the older generation.

Someone whose partner has died becomes the sole decision-maker. They may find themselves having to take on tasks they have little or no experience of.

John had never managed the finances.

Betty didn't know anything about gardening.

When an eldest child dies, the second one becomes the eldest. How does that make them feel?

After the death of her sister, Harriet realised:

'A major thing was the position my sister held in the family: of enabling people in the family to relate to each other, like with grandparents. I suddenly realised that I was in that role now.'

If one of two siblings die, the remaining one becomes an only child. They may find it particularly hard going on family holidays.

Sometimes, when one parent dies at a young age, the eldest son or daughter feels they have to step into that vacant role. This may not be appropriate; and may place a big burden on that child. Adult children still living at home find themselves acting as carer and sometimes give up their own career in order to do this.

> When her father died, Jean moved into the role of carer for her mother, who had dementia. It felt as if their relationship had reversed, and she had become the mother.

An innocent question can hook into the emotional struggles that come about from these changes.

About two years after Daniel died I was asked, in a group situation, 'How many children do you have?' That question threw me. After a pregnant pause, when I felt I was caught in the undergrowth, I answered 'I've got three, but I did have four.' Even now after eleven years, I still find that question difficult. I now have three boys living, but if I say 'three' I feel I am not acknowledging that once I had four. To me he is still part of our family. However, if I let the person know that one of my sons has died, then that opens up the way for more questions which I may not wish to answer. Particularly in the early days, depending how I felt emotionally, I was not always able to cope with talking about him.

Andrew, whose eldest child died shortly after birth, echoed this sentiment about thirteen years later.

> 'I dread being asked the seemingly innocent question, "How many children do you have?" Should I be honest and say two? Arthur is still so alive for me it always seems like a betrayal. I'll always have three children.'

Bereavement may become a time for us to 'take stock' of our lives.

> David retired shortly after his wife died. He felt he needed to make changes in his life.

Maybe death also causes us to face up to our own mortality and consider our priorities. Perhaps subconsciously we begin to think about things we wish we had experienced or achieved. Maybe the circumstances leading up to the death had prevented us from following our dreams, or limited what we were able to do. We may change our career or lifestyle, or engage in a new hobby.

These changes may be for other reasons. Having a new focus may give us some respite from continually thinking about the death. They may help us in coming to terms with what has happened.

> Gwen travelled the world after her son died. She felt it gave her space and time to adjust.

Yet this may be a way of escaping from that reality.

> After their daughter died, Tom and Heather kept going on holiday, because they could not face being in the house with all the memories.

At the beginning of this book, I mentioned that I started on a degree course two years after Daniel died. It felt good to have something different to focus on and to have a new challenge. I realised that he would never reach his potential, but I had an opportunity to reach mine. Whether I would have undertaken the course if Daniel had lived, I don't know. Without Daniel to support, I had more time available, but it was actually other circumstances which led me to consider doing a course of study. However it felt as if something positive had come out of Daniel's death: as if I was doing it as a tribute to him.

In the previous chapter we looked at how friendships can be affected by bereavement: maybe permanently, or maybe temporarily, while adjustments are made. However we may find that our social circle changes. A widower who used to go to a social event with his wife may find it difficult to continue going on his own. Couples who used to meet together, find that it is not the same when one of them is missing.

> My parents used to regularly visit some friends, but after my father died, my mother stopped getting invited to their house and the friendship drifted until there was no contact.

Some people find that they withdraw socially for a while: they are so consumed by their grief. Usually they will pick up the threads again gradually.

There are other aspects of change caused by the death of someone close to us. This may be tied up with having to work

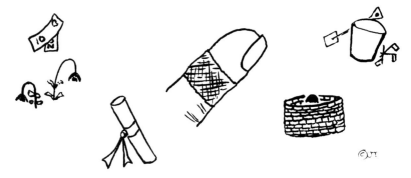

out who we are now in terms of our role. How do we suddenly change our thinking about how we perceive ourselves? How can we suddenly begin living a different sort of life?

Elsie said:

> 'I felt I stuck out like a sore thumb; I wasn't a wife any longer: I didn't know who I was any more.'

> Deidre had a friend who she went on holiday with every year. They also spent much of their leisure time together. Her friend became ill and died. She suddenly felt very lonely. So now she goes on organised group holidays and has joined various clubs.

Hazel, widowed in her early sixties, remarked:

> 'I've been living as a married person for nearly thirty years. I've been part of a couple. Now I have to learn to live as a single person again.'

Some couples spend all their leisure time together, so when one of them dies, this will be an added issue for them to cope with. The interests they had may not be suitable to continue with as a single person. For instance, they may have played tennis in a foursome or spent evenings playing Scrabble together. They may not have the confidence to continue with some of their social activities on their own. This leaves a big gap socially and emotionally, as well as creating many empty hours to fill.

> Ian and I have always had interests and activities that we do on our own, as well as those we do together. If one of us dies suddenly while we are still fit and active, those parts of our lives could stay the same.

Bereavement brings about a variety of changes. No two people are the same. It may be difficult to say how the death has changed us, but we know that it has. The circumstances and relationships involved may have a bearing on this. For some the pain is so great that they 'build a wall' around themselves as a protection against being hurt again. Others feel more vulnerable. Depending on the cause of death, and whether the person has come to terms with it, their reaction may result in them becoming hard and feeling vengeful. Alternatively they may become more sensitive to others pain.

> Susan referred to 'the person she was before'.

Duncan and Jane, many years after the death of their young sister, reflected,

'It's made us the people we are and has given us more sensitivity and compassion.'

For Pru, after the death of her father, came the realisation that:

'Life is so precious, and it's too precious to be out of relationship with people.'

We Are Seven

—A simple Child,
That lightly draws its breath,
And feels its life in every limb,
What should it know of death?

I met a little cottage Girl:
She was eight years old, she said;
Her hair was thick with many a curl
That clustered round her head.

She had a rustic, woodland air,
And she was wildly clad:
Her eyes were fair, and very fair;
—Her beauty made me glad.

'Sisters and brothers, little Maid,
How many may you be?'
'How many? Seven in all,' she said
And wondering looked at me.

'And where are they? I pray you tell.'
She answered, 'Seven are we;
And two of us at Conway dwell,
And two are gone to sea.

'Two of us in the church-yard lie,
My sister and my brother;
And, in the church-yard cottage, I
Dwell near them with my mother.'

'You say that two at Conway dwell,
And two are gone to sea,
Yet ye are seven!—I pray you tell,
Sweet Maid, how this may be.'

Then did the little Maid reply,
'Seven boys and girls are we;
Two of us in the church-yard lie,
Beneath the church-yard tree.'

'You run about, my little Maid,
Your limbs they are alive;
If two are in the church-yard laid,
Then ye are only five.'

'Their graves are green, they may be seen,'
The little Maid replied,
'Twelve steps or more from my mother's door,
And they are side by side.

'My stockings there I often knit,
My kerchief there I hem;
And there upon the ground I sit,
And sing a song to them.

'And often after sunset, Sir,
When it is light and fair,
I take my little porringer,
And eat my supper there.

'The first that died was sister Jane;
In bed she moaning lay,
Till God released her of her pain;
And then she went away.

'So in the church-yard she was laid;
And, when the grass was dry,
Together round her grave we played,
My brother John and I.

'And when the ground was white with snow,
And I could run and slide,
My brother John was forced to go,
And he lies by her side.'

'How many are you, then,' said I,
'If they two are in heaven?'
Quick was the little Maid's reply,
'O Master! we are seven.'

'But they are dead; those two are dead!
Their spirits are in heaven!'
'Twas throwing words away; for still
The little Maid would have her will,
And said, 'Nay, we are seven!'

(William Wordsworth)

Chapter Thirteen
Keeping the Memory Alive

When someone special to us dies, we continue to remember them. There is a sense in which we still want to connect with them even though they aren't physically with us any more. Will I, one day, forget what Daniel's voice used to sound like? We want to be able to acknowledge and keep alive the part they have played in our lives. How we do this will be different for everyone.

One way of remembering and keeping the memory alive is to visit the grave or place where the ashes are buried or scattered. This may also be part of the grieving journey. Sometimes the one who is mourning will go regularly to 'chat' to the person who has died. Others may go at special family times as a way of feeling close to them and feeling, that in a way they are still including them.

We all cope differently. Family members must allow each other to grieve and remember in the way that is right for them. Some people do not feel a need to visit the grave at all. Ian has never been to the cemetery since we buried Daniel's ashes, while I go from time to time. Sometimes I go on my own and sometimes I take a friend with me. Ian would come with me if I asked him, but I know that he does not feel a need to go and I respect that. One of our sons went on his own, probably more than two years after Daniel died, and now feels he does not need to go again. However, two years ago his wife felt a need to go, and they went together.

Sally struggled with visiting the grave of her stillborn son as she felt she could not cope with it. It was too painful, and the emotions were still too raw. However, her husband wanted to go, and there was the unspoken pressure of feeling it was the expected thing to do. 'What sort of a mother will people think I am if I don't go and visit my son's grave?' Now, many years later, it is not an issue and Sally is happy to visit.

Similarly, I have sometimes wondered if there are those who think we do not care, because there are no flowers where Daniel's ashes are buried.

Graham's son is buried near his home. He visits the grave every day, and wonders why his son's widow only comes periodically. Does he think she is not grieving? Maybe she does not feel a need to visit. In any event, she has a long journey on public transport to get there, which makes it difficult for her.

We must be careful not to assume that people do not care enough, or are not upset, if they do not show their grief in the same way that we do. People visit the grave for a variety of reasons.

So how do we keep the memories alive? How do we stop the person from becoming like a book on a shelf that gathers dust and is never read? We don't want to blot them out of our memories, as if they had never existed.

Often the person who has died will have left certain of their belongings to people who have been special to them. Or after the funeral we may be asked if there is anything in the house that we would like to have, in memory of them.

We have ornaments and plants in our home which remind me of certain friends and family every time I look at them.

Of course, the memories they evoke may be a mixture of happy and sad ones.

Many people have photos around the house, giving a constant feeling of closeness to those who have died. Some people have their own, personal, symbolic memorial to a loved one.

In our garden we have planted two box plants to grow round the bike frame which was on Daniel's coffin. We can see it from our kitchen window. When I trim it during the summer, I find myself thinking about him. We have also planted a shrub in a big pot given by his uncle and we refer to it as 'Daniel's shrub'. There is a stone with his name inscribed on it, in the pot.

Some people have special places where they go to help them feel close to the person who has died, or to help them on their journey.

Heather goes to a garden where there is a tree planted in her husband's memory.

Maureen returned to the place where her husband died while they were on holiday. Friends were anxious for her, but it proved to be a healing time.

Visiting the grave, or place where ashes have been scattered or buried, is a comfort to many. Some people keep the ashes in the house, where they can see them all the time.

There are now woods where trees can be planted in memory of someone who has died: a living, lasting memorial.

Some people make the anniversary of the death a special occasion. We decided as a family that we would focus on Daniel's birth date which was obviously a happy time. So each year we have arranged a day out together as a family. For the first few years, on his birthday, two of our boys went cycling together in the forest where Daniel lived, and where he loved to cycle.

Susan's family always light a candle for their daughter at Christmas.

In a previous chapter I mentioned how we can feel ambushed by unexpected reminders that throw us back into our grief. On the other hand, once the initial emotional shock of the ambush has passed we may find ourselves remembering happy occasions. We may be able to turn that experience into a positive way of keeping the memory alive.

So when I see a mountain-biker wearing a black cap I can also recall how much Daniel enjoyed cycling in the forest, and how that was probably the happiest time in his adult life.

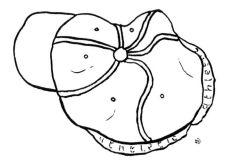

Being able to bring the deceased person into the conversation in a natural way can be helpful. You may be watching a new film and comment that they would have enjoyed seeing it. We have two friends who keep Daniel's memory alive for us in special ways. One always sends a greetings card and a letter during July, the month of his birth and death. The other still brings him into our conversations and asks me how I am. I find it comforting that they both acknowledge that Daniel's death will always be with us.

In recent years, hospices have organised Light up a Life community events in November or December, to remember loved ones who have died. Often there is the opportunity to light a candle or hang a message on a tree. Some churches hold special services as an act of remembrance.

My own experience of this is that several years ago I went to one such service with a friend whose husband had died the year before. They were very special friends to our family and I found it very comforting and helpful. However I had the opportunity to attend one several years after Daniel had died and could not even cope with the idea of it. Just knowing it was taking place unsettled me because I could only think of it in terms of Daniel, even though so many other friends and family had died. I felt as though it would take me back to a grieving place that I did not wish to return to.

Those who have died are a part of our history, maybe of our family. They will always be somewhere in our lives. They have influenced who we were; and who we have become. It feels natural for me to bring Daniel into our conversation, although there will always be a sadness that he is no longer with us.

Maybe, too, there will always be that longing to have him back. Hopefully, we will eventually find a comfortable place for our loved ones in our hearts and minds.

Chapter Fourteen
Daniel

A newspaper recently reported the death of a sixteen-year-old boy who had taken ecstasy. His mother said that he had never taken drugs before. It was not the kind of thing he did.

She continued, 'I want people to know that's not who he is.' I can empathise with that mother, as that is what I want to say when I tell people the cause of Daniel's death. I want to tell them that the facts relating to his death will probably make them come to the wrong conclusion as to what sort of person he was. I want them to know his story.

Daniel was born in 1975, the first of our four boys. He was a happy little boy who loved playing and being outdoors. However, school was a difficult time for him, and he struggled all through those years of education. Most of his teachers acknowledged that there was something wrong. He was assessed by various medical and educational specialists. No-one seemed to be able to identify the problem so there was no help available. Perhaps if he had been born today the situation would have been different, as there is now more awareness of learning difficulties. Many of the everyday social skills that we took for granted with his three brothers just did not seem to be on his agenda. His communication skills seemed lacking.

My memories of Daniel's late teens and early twenties are mostly ones of sadness and difficulty for us all. He became estranged from us even while still living at home. Some of his friends were not helpful to him. Without going into detail I will just say that he used drugs for a while and got on the wrong side of the law several times.

Yet there was a soft side to his character. When Daniel was seven we had some friends living with us for a while. After Daniel's death, one of their adult sons wrote:

'I have good memories of the time we spent with you, particularly from Daniel with his gentle nature and sense of fun.'

I remember him coming out with me, in his twenties, when I was looking after a young girl with learning disabilities. They walked hand in hand round the town. Later still when we used to go for walks in the woods, he would hold my hand and help me over muddy or difficult patches.

Daniel had a friend who worked with youngsters with Attention Deficit Hyperactivity Disorder. One day Daniel came home and said he felt he had many of the difficulties they had. His friend had advised him to see his doctor, which he did. That was the start of him being under the care of a psychiatrist, Alan. We learned then that he was suffering from depression, and probably had been for many years.

When Daniel was born he had lost a small amount of oxygen, due to the cord being wrapped twice round his neck. Alan believed, purely from his years of experience, that such children were affected by this problem at birth. Initially they seem to manage and then as time goes by they are unable to cope with life. It was not until several years later that Daniel told us that he had felt anxious for as long as he could remember. We had not realised the extent of this as he was growing up.

Holding down a job for any length of time became a problem. However, most of the time he managed to stay in work. He tried living independently but ended up coming home as he could not cope. I remember him asking me why one of his friends could cope on his own and he couldn't. There was a part of him that didn't seem to mature properly. He still wanted to go out and play: on his bike, or his roller blades, and he still had a box of Lego. One of his brothers described him as having 'a bit of his brain that didn't seem to be wired properly'.

After a particular two-year period when Daniel was back at home, depressed, not working, and spending most of the day in bed, he disappeared for several days. He did this from time to time. When he came back, in time for an appointment with Alan, we learned that he had gone to stay with a friend in another town. His friend said that he could stay with him and his family if he got himself a job. That was the beginning of him turning his life around; although it was sometimes two steps forward and one step back. Daniel later told us that he knew he would never sort himself out while he stayed in his home town. We will always be grateful to that friend for giving him the opportunity he needed. It was also the start of him 'coming back into the family' and beginning to talk and share with us in a way that he had never been able to do before.

Daniel lived in that town for several years, during which time, he moved and had various jobs and living accommodation. Eventually he ended up working in a small brewery, which he loved, and would proudly tell people that he was a brewer. Some of the beer he brewed won awards.

However, the combination of drinking too much and depression setting in again led to him not doing his job properly. His boss supported him in an amazing way and arranged for him to see a counsellor. Alison was just right for Daniel. She seemed to understand him and how he 'ticked,' and he made so much progress with her. He began to understand himself. His feelings of self-worth began to change slowly for the better. Daniel came home again for support and we were driving him to and from work each day. We knew that he wanted to be back living there and we felt that he needed the stability of having a home of his own. So we bought a house together. He was excited about the changes he could make to it, to 'put his own stamp on it'.

However, by the time the sale was completed Daniel had been signed off work as the depression took hold again. On the day he was due to move, he stayed in bed, and remained there for several days. One of his brothers offered to get a temporary job and move with him to help him settle in. He stayed for three months. I will always feel that gesture was a very special gift to Daniel, especially knowing he was not easy to live with. His brothers and we saw him frequently. As he got to know his neighbours they would look out for him. One of them would phone us if she was particularly concerned about him. She would take him meals if he was not eating. He was still having support from Alison and Alan.

Over the next twelve months or so Daniel gradually improved. Another good friend lent him his dog, which meant he had company. It also meant he had to get up to take her out, although we know that she was neglected at times. He also spent many hours cycling in the local forest, which he had grown to love. The house was a 'work in progress,' as he drew plans for furniture and fitments that he wanted to make. We saw some of them become a reality. At times it looked like a builder's yard but it didn't matter. It was his house, and he had goals to work towards.

During this time, Daniel talked about his difficulties, and his desire to be able to cope with his life. One of the things he wanted to sort out was his inability to say 'no' to people. This helped us to understand why he had left several of his jobs. In most cases, he had been offered more responsibility, which he did not feel he could cope with. As he could not say 'no,' his way of handling that situation was to leave. This applied to social occasions as well, when he would say 'yes' to an invitation and then not turn up.

About a year before he died, Daniel was referred to a psychologist, who talked with him, and gave him various tests to look at how his brain functioned. They showed up various difficulties. She felt that she could help him with strategies for coping, but sadly this had not been put in place before he died.

The day came when Daniel felt he was fit enough to return to work. The brewery had not been able to keep his job open indefinitely, but he had hoped that one day he would be able to return there. In the meantime, he was accepted by a local firm of wholesalers to work in their warehouse. They knew of his mental health problems and that he had not worked for about eighteen months. However they were willing to employ him to get him back into the work-place. Daniel had been for a couple of trial days, which he had enjoyed, and was waiting for a phone call to say when he could start. He was looking forward to working again, knowing that he would just be able to do what was asked of him and then go home.

I arranged to spend a day with him before starting his new job. We went shopping, to look for a new tent, which he helped to choose. Then we had lunch at a nearby garden centre, and bought a garden bench in memory of my mother. When we got back to his home, he offered to make us dinner which must have been the first time ever so it was a very special day. As I left, he gave me a big hug. I said, 'Look after yourself' and he gave me a grin and said, 'I will.'

Three days later he was dead.

The autopsy showed that he died from the toxic effects of alcohol, anti-depressants and methadone. A friend, who was staying with him that weekend, was taking prescription methadone. At the inquest we listened to his version of the events of that night and so understood the facts of his death. However, for us, the 'whys and wherefores' of that night will always remain a mystery.

Chapter Fifteen
Remembering Daniel

Often, when we read accounts in the paper or hear in the news of people dying, we learn positive, good things about them and their lives. There will be quotes from work colleagues and neighbours about their good character, and how they will be sorely missed. If a child has died we hear about how friendly and helpful they were, and how they were such a pleasure to teach. When we attend funerals we usually hear stories of special times with family, and of unknown good deeds. We hear tributes from friends and family. There will be those touched by the life of the deceased in ways we knew nothing about, Funny incidents are retold. We come away with good memories, and a warm feeling towards them.

Yet there are people who may have only a few happy memories to look back on. They may struggle to remember the good times, may feel ashamed of the lifestyle of the deceased person. Still others may have been estranged from the one who has died.

We read of parents learning of a daughter's death and then discovering that she had been a prostitute. We hear of drug addicts dying from taking an overdose and see pictures of them in squalid living conditions. Parents may find it hard to recall that moment when they first saw their child as a tiny baby with all the potential and dreams they encompassed. People die in prison. They may have parents, children, siblings or a partner. Good memories may not come to mind easily. Do we sometimes forget that because of those deaths there are families somewhere who are grieving? Often we focus on the cause of the death or the lifestyle of the one who has died. Our own thoughts and attitudes can detract from the suffering of those who mourn.

When there are difficult circumstances to come to terms with, grieving families may find it hard to be able to share their grief.

Where do they look for support? When a family member has been found in the home after committing suicide, it must be hard to continue living there with that memory. After Daniel died, I could not cope going into his house for many months.

It was a long time before the heartache of some of Daniel's life faded in my thoughts. After he told us how he had been anxious for as long as he could remember, I kept imagining him as a sad little boy. I had to get past that picture, and the one of him as an adult, struggling to cope with life. I had always loved him, but I needed to find those good memories. I needed to remember the special moments and achievements, and not just the failures and the difficulties of his life.

I mentioned earlier how he seemed lacking in the social etiquettes which our other boys had grown up with and which most of us take for granted. So it was a big day when, as an adult, he said 'thank you' when we gave him a lift in the car. It was good when we visited him in his home and he asked us if we would like a cup of tea. It was a 'wow' moment when he told us he had started taking an interest in football so that he could discuss it with his neighbour. It was special when, a few days before he died, he phoned one of his brothers to thank him and his wife for the birthday present they had sent him. That particular 'thank you' was a 'first'; and they spoke for about two hours, which had also never happened before.

I'm pleased that I can remember the sensitive part of him. When I walk past a certain church I remember that he used to remove the slow worms for Julia when she was tending the garden. He knew she didn't like them. I remember how upset he was at his grandmother's funeral. He hadn't seen her for some considerable time but I think the service reminded him of good times he had spent with her. He would always play and have patience with a friend's son who had learning difficulties. Maybe he empathised with his struggles. I have a card with a tiny bear pin attached to it, which I keep on the dressing table. The wording includes 'So pin this Bear Hug on you and wherever you may be, remember that he always bears a Bear Hug just from me!' Not what you would expect from a twenty-eight year-old. I like to think that they express what he wasn't able to say. He gave us the report from the psychologist, which included things he had told her about himself, and how he knew that it had been hard for us as his parents. Again, I think that was his way of sharing his thoughts with us.

I can think back now, and see that his work history was not all bad. He was offered the job at the brewery because the owner had seen him at work in a pub and realised he was good mathematically. The job involved formulae and ratios. One of his former work colleagues sought him out to offer him employment.

I can also look back and remember incidents and situations that make me remember his capabilities. As a young lad he stayed calm and fetched help when a child fell off a climbing frame where we were camping. The paramedics praised him for 'doing the right things'. For a while he built cycle wheels for a specialist bike company. When he worked in a bike shop, the owner described his knowledge as 'encyclopaedic'. I can feel proud of the furniture he had made for his home, and the plans he had for it. When I'm working in the kitchen, I remember that it was Daniel who assembled some of the units when we refitted it. I recall the many times that he helped his brothers and friends with wiring up stereo systems in their cars.

Even when he had been badly depressed he always wanted to get back to work, once he began to feel better. When someone at work was stealing, he went to his boss and told him of his past. That must have taken some courage. How good for him to know that his boss respected him for that, and to be assured that they knew it wasn't him. He said he wanted to tell the culprit not to do it because 'it wasn't worth it'.

There are times to remember that made us laugh. One day, he took a neighbour's dog for a walk and brought him back dripping wet and covered in this black stuff that was sticking to his fur. He had jumped into a stagnant pond. How we laughed as he hosed the dog down: all to no avail! He had to return the dog and confess! We have a photo on our wall of Daniel and one of his brothers, as young children, in a very large hole in the garden.

They spent weeks digging it. His brother has said since, that he always wondered what the hole was for? We laugh and say, 'it was just a hole.' Another time when they were together in the garden, the same brother got covered in mud, so Daniel hosed him down. He looked as if he had been in a mud bath, but he was still smiling!

Maybe my last proud memory was at the inquest, when the coroner read out that he was a 'well-nourished male'. He had learned to look after himself.

These are only a few examples of life with Daniel that have helped me to see the whole person: to see him for who he was. When life is difficult it is easy for the good things to get overlooked or forgotten. He was a complicated person and maybe I never really understood him. However I'm so glad that latterly, there were times that have left happy memories. He did not like Christmas, usually spending it in bed, but his last one was spent with one of his brothers and sister-in-law. They visited family friends and he was able to play with their boys and say how much he had enjoyed that Christmas.

Shortly before he died we all went to a wedding and we have lovely photos of him, looking so happy and relaxed. However, most importantly for me is knowing that for the last few years of his life he enjoyed being part of his family again.

'And when the stream that overflows has passed,
A consciousness remains upon the silent shore of memory;
Images and precious thoughts that shall not be
And cannot be destroyed.'

(William Wordsworth, from *The Excursion*)

Chapter Sixteen
A Different Kind of Bereavement

There are other kinds of bereavement, as well as that caused by someone's death.

When we know that someone has been 'bereaved,' we often refer to their 'loss'. Both these words are used in the sense of having been deprived of something, or of ceasing to have. So we have loss of life, but also of many other things which impact severely on our lives. I will not discuss any of these in depth as there is other literature on these subjects. I just want to touch on a few of the more common areas of loss.

There is the loss of a job through illness, retirement, or redundancy. Our employment may have taken up a big percentage of our time. What will take its place? We may have been in the same job for many years. It may have been our reason for getting up in the morning. Our colleagues may have become our friends. Will this continue? Some people think of themselves in terms of their role. 'I'm retiring from teaching' so who, or what, will I be then? It may feel like a loss of identity.

Parents may experience many different kinds of loss as their children pass through various stages in their lives. That first day of school: no longer a toddler. Transferring from primary to senior school: the end of early childhood. There is a sense of loss when our children start becoming independent and don't need us in the same way as when they were younger. Then, when they leave home, there is more feeling of loss.

Moving house can be difficult, especially if you have lived in that house for many years, and so many memories are tied up in it. A friend who was having to think about moving house locally to down-size said that she did not want to live where she would have to walk past her old house. If the move is to a different area then the number of things that will be 'lost' will be greater: all the familiar people, places and social activities. We feel the loss when friends move away, particularly if they are friends we have spent much time with. Other similar losses may be from Day Centres, clubs and other groups closing down, leaving a big gap in people's lives.

When a couple divorce or separate there is bereavement. Just as a stone thrown into a pond sends ripples, so the effect of divorce may spread out to friends and family alike. There is the loss of relationship for the couple themselves. Children no longer have their family unit. The home, financial security, the wider family, such as grandparents, social standing, are just some of the losses that may occur. It may feel like a 'sudden death' for some members of the family, if there had been no opportunity to say 'goodbye' and no chance of meeting up again. The ramifications of divorce or separation are too complex to discuss here.

At the beginning of this book I referred to my mother being in residential care. This was a new experience for me. I had visited people in homes before but had no personal experience of all that being 'in care' involved. Today there are many elderly people living in residential care. I sometimes wonder if enough thought is given to the impact this has on the people who have given up their independence and home. Is their loss acknowledged, and are they given the opportunity to work through their feelings of bereavement? Sometimes this change in their lives happens after they have lost their lifelong partner, so they are already journeying with grief when they have to cope with another loss. Sometimes, their children move them away from the area where they have lived, depriving them of friends who would like to visit them.

Less tangible is the loss of something that 'might have been': of potential. Children born with disabilities lose the future that they might have had, and which their parents may have hoped for them. For those who die at a young age, there is the knowledge, for those who mourn, that there will be no career, no children, no grandchildren, no fulfilment of dreams. This also applies to couples who would like a family but are unable to conceive. They need to be allowed to mourn for their loss. This will also affect the wider family, who may have looked forward to becoming grandparents, uncles or other relation. Even though there are now other ways in which couples are able to have a family, there will still be that initial grieving. There is also a grieving by the birth families when children are adopted. Deteriorating health is like a bereavement, as the sufferer comes to terms with several different losses that may be incurred by the illness. Similarly when friends or relatives become estranged, there is a sense of bereavement.

So we see that grief is something that affects us all to a greater or lesser degree. Throughout life we are faced with endings: some of which will be traumatic, while others will not seem worth mentioning. Endings deprive us of something, whether tangible or not: the end of a life, the end of our dreams. I remember one of our university lecturers saying that some students would experience grief when their course ended: not something we would normally associate with someone who has just gained a degree. Loss affects us all differently. We need to allow ourselves and others time to mourn and to walk through that valley. It may be a long trek or a short hike.

Chapter Seventeen
My Story

During the last few years I have read many books and journals on the subject of death and bereavement. There are differing theories and understandings of grief and how to work your way through it. Nearly all seem to say that bereavement from the death of a child is the hardest to come to terms with.

It's the wrong way round: parents don't expect to organise and attend their own child's funeral.

During my adult life I have experienced the death of my parents, work colleagues, relatives and very special friends. Yet I have to say that none of them have evoked the deep and raw emotion in me that Daniel's death did. None of them caused such distress, that at times seemed more than I could bear. I am not saying that only the death of a child can cause such grief, but that is how it was for me.

It is now eleven years since Daniel died. Am I still walking along that dark valley? On the whole: 'no'. I feel that I have emerged into the sunshine at the end; but sometimes I find myself returning to it briefly.

I have already referred to the many people I have heard utter sentiments such as:

'You don't get over it, you learn to live with it.'

I would say that I have learned to live without Daniel, but I'm sure the sadness I feel because he has died will always be with me. I'm sure I will always miss him, and I feel that a part of me has died with him. I still get 'ambushed' from time to time, incurring that return to the valley. It can feel like a dark cloud about to burst but usually it's only a short heavy shower. I am learning to turn those times into positive memories. So all of that is still with me as I continue on my life's journey.

Whenever there was some perceived difficulty, Daniel would say, 'Oh it'll be alright' and I've often imagined him saying that to us since he died. So now I'm doing the things I used to do before, have developed new skills and begun different activities. I feel that mostly I'm out of that particular valley and enjoying the varied countryside which will always have its 'ups and downs'.

Yes, there are still things I struggle with and maybe there always will be. About two years ago, one of our boys went to live near where Daniel lived. I found it hard driving past what had been his house and going to the same shops that he had frequented. Now and again our children send us new photos of themselves. Each time, I am faced with the fact that there will be no new photos of Daniel. He will always be thirty-one. In a sense he has gone from being the eldest to being the youngest.

I mentioned in an earlier chapter that some bereaved people feel the death has changed them. When I see youngsters struggling to find jobs or being homeless, I now have a much greater feeling of empathy for them. Not everyone has a good support network. I think how Daniel could so easily have ended up 'on the streets' at certain times in his life, if he hadn't had his family around him. It has also made me value and want to nurture relationships more. Life is so fragile.

From earlier comments, readers may have realised that I am a Christian. I have found my trust in God has brought comfort. I believe God has the bigger picture. Looking back at the events leading up to Daniel's death, I can see God's hand in them: almost as if God was putting things in place to help us in our grief.

Daniel died at a time when it seemed he was getting his life together and learning to value himself. He had made such good progress with Alison, his counsellor, and was looking forward to going back to work. He told us of his plans for finishing his lounge in time for Christmas. He seemed happy and contented. I think I would have found it harder to come to terms with his death if he had been in the depths of despair, as he had been in the past.

I have already referred to the wedding we went to shortly before he died. The couple had decided to get married after living together for several years. As a result of that we have many photos and memories of a happy family day: the only up-to-date pictures we had of him.

The day I spent with Daniel the week he died has left me with special memories.

After the service in the crematorium, we stood round his coffin and I had my arms round two of our other boys, who stood one on each side of me. A few days later we received a hand-made card with some words from the Bible, saying, 'As a mother comforts her child, so will I comfort you'. How appropriate.

I found it difficult to cope with the thought of Daniel dying on his own, even though his friend was in the house. What sort of death did he have? A doctor told us that he would have just gone to sleep and his organs would have closed down so he wouldn't have suffered. I also hold on to the fact that Daniel would have said he was having a good weekend with a friend.

I have not asked the question. 'Why did God allow this to happen?.' There is no answer. I do know that Alan thought that Daniel would always have bouts of depression that may have worsened with each one. He may always have needed support and one day we wouldn't have been there to give it to him. God does not say that we will not have troubles and difficulties. There will always be illness, death, job-loss, and other such events which are part of life. What I do know is that God has promised to walk with us and be there for us.

So our life has returned to a normal that has changed, because one person who we expected to be sharing it with, isn't here any more: Daniel.

Chapter Eighteen
An Ending

So how does this journey with grief end? Does it end?

When travelling in the car, children often ask how long the journey is going to take. We may hear 'Are we nearly there?' several times before we reach the end of our journey. Similarly people often ask how long grieving lasts? I have been told and read that it can be anything from two to ten years. Do we really know? I have heard several people say that the second year after the death was worse than the first. Is that because the first year is taken up with so many practicalities and adjustments that the reality doesn't really sink in till then?

We too may want to know if we're nearly there. Initially it may feel as if we haven't got a destination, so we don't know if we are nearly there.

In chapter one I mentioned some of the expressions I have heard and read about in relation to how bereavement is perceived. Our grief is something to 'get over,' 'recover or move on from'. We are expected to 'let go' of our loved one, or have 'closure' on our grief.

What does all this mean?

I think the intense sorrow, which dominates our whole being initially, lessens for most people after an indefinite time. The depth of feelings of grief will continue to change and fluctuate. Also, as we have seen, we can be transported back to that distressing time even after many years. If we feel stuck in that intense grief and unable to see a way forward, it may be helpful to seek professional advice and support.

It may be helpful to talk with a counsellor anyway. About eighteen months after Daniel died, I suddenly felt a great need to talk with someone outside the situation: someone not emotionally involved. I needed to sort through the thoughts and feelings that had arisen from Daniel's death. I talked with my doctor who thought it would be a good idea and then I referred myself to one of our local counselling services. It was helpful to have someone listen while I voiced all that was on my mind and in my heart. Sometimes my counsellor would challenge what I said or put a different slant on things. Other times she would gently encourage or tell me that what I felt was normal. Somehow it enabled me to feel more at peace and able to carry on towards the new 'normal'.

To say that we have closure implies, to me, that our grief has ended or resolved. Yet when we emerge from that valley, we still take our sorrow with us. We have the rest of life's journey to walk; and we take our loved one with us. They are a part of us. We let them go, in the sense that we accept their death, but we carry them with us in our hearts.

There comes a time when we can laugh again, take an interest in other people and things. Most of us can go back to work and resume some, if not all, of the lifestyle we had before. However there may be some activities or friendships that we feel unable to take up again.

I believe we will always remember the person who has died. If the death was a difficult one, hopefully that will fade into the background as happier memories take their place. The acute pain will lessen as we adjust and adapt to not having them as a tangible part of our lives. Our deep sense of loss may stay with us, but will not necessarily debilitate us in the way it did at the beginning. We learn to remember without the pain of earlier days. Somehow we integrate our feelings and our loss into the person we are now. We find that comfortable place within ourselves for our loved one to rest.

No matter how well or otherwise we cope with bereavement, we have to acknowledge that life won't go back to how it was before. Death sometimes changes how we view life and its priorities. It is often a defining moment in time when we think in terms of 'before' and 'after'. The characters in the story have changed; and as Andrew said, 'it's a different landscape.' We may even feel like a different person: that we won't go back to being who we were before.

I have been writing this book now for several years. During that time, the conversations I have had, both recently and in the past, the books I have read, and my own experience, have shaped my thoughts about bereavement. I think the valley is the beginning of our walk with grief and that the journey continues throughout the rest of our lives. Physically we all walk at different speeds, and we often take different routes to get to the same destination. Sometimes we need to stop and rest before continuing our journey. So it is with grieving. We have to learn how fast to walk and which way to take. We have to learn how to navigate those tough areas: how to deal with being ambushed. In time, we hope to reach that place where we can live in harmony with our loss.

If you are the one who is grieving I hope that what you have read will help you find that place. If you are the one who is 'walking alongside' a grieving friend, then I hope it will enable you to give support with understanding and compassion as you travel that road together.

There are no easy answers to 'walking with grief'. You may not agree with everything I have written. Some of our experiences will differ; others will be similar. However I trust that my observations and practical suggestions will be of some help as you walk this journey.

'We must allow each other to grieve differently.'

'Life will get back to normal but normal will be different.'

Helpful Information

For what to do after someone dies, go to:
https://www.gov.uk/browse/births-deaths-marriages/death

Age UK gives information about benefits. Your local office can be found at www.ageuk.org.uk

Your local undertaker will be able to give you information regarding green and woodland burial sites.

Helpful Books

A comprehensive book list on bereavement can be found at
http://www.hospiceofamador.org/images/PDFs/Bereavement_
Book_List.pdf

Acknowledgements

Thank you to all who have had any input into this book. I have included many personal stories that I have heard over the years, but I have changed the names and the details to protect the anonymity of those concerned.

My special thanks go to Sarah, as without her help and encouragement, this book would not have been written.

Thank you to my husband Ian, who has kept me supplied with numerous cups of coffee and meals while writing this book.

Thanks also to:

Alison, who said, 'You and Ian will grieve differently. That's alright. You need to allow each other to do that.'

We have.

John, who told one of our boys at Daniel's funeral, 'Life will get back to normal: but normal will be different.'

It has and it is.